NEW MERMAIDS

General editors:
William C. Carroll, Boston University
Brian Gibbons, University of Münster
Tiffany Stern, University of Oxford

Reconstructi

NEW MERMAIDS

NEW MERMAIDS

JOHN GAY

THE BEGGAR'S OPERA

Edited by Vivien Jones
and David Lindley
University of Leeds

Methuen Drama • London

New Mermaids

1 3 5 7 9 10 8 6 4 2

New Mermaid edition first published 2010

Methuen Drama
A & C Black Publishers Limited
36 Soho Square
London W1D 3QY
www.methuendrama.com

ISBN: 978 0 7136 7382 1

A CIP catalogue record for this book is
available from the British Library

Typeset by Country Setting, Kingsdown, Kent CT14 8ES
Printed in the UK by CPI Cox & Wyman, Reading, RG1 8EX

CONTENTS

ACKNOWLEDGEMENTS

We are grateful to a number of people for assistance in the preparation of this edition. Robert Jones and Jeremy Barlow each offered valuable information about the early performances of *The Beggar's Opera*. The archives of the Royal Shakespeare Company at the Shakespeare Centre in Stratford and the National Theatre in London provided essential material about modern performances, and our thanks go to their extremely helpful staff, and to that of our 'home' library, the Brotherton Library of Leeds University, the source of the photograph of the title page. Simon Trussler patiently assisted with the production of the music. To the General Editors, Brian Gibbons and Tiffany Stern, we owe much, both for their patience in the long gestation of the edition, and for suggestions and corrections along the way.

Vivien Jones, David Lindley
Leeds, August 2009

INTRODUCTION

About the Play

John Gay's *Beggar's Opera* was a theatrical sensation when it was first produced at the Theatre Royal in Lincoln's Inn Fields in January 1728. In that first season it ran for a record sixty-two nights; it was the play most often performed throughout the eighteenth century and it continued to be revived until the 1880s; in the twentieth century it inspired adaptations by writers as various as Bertolt Brecht, in his *Threepenny Opera*, and Alan Ayckbourn.[1] The play's early success was partly due to its novelty. Gay invented a new dramatic form, the ballad opera, which combined spoken dialogue with songs based on familiar and much-loved tunes – in effect, the first musical. The result was a play which appealed immediately to a wide audience. But its success was also a matter of content. Set in London's underworld, *The Beggar's Opera* is a devastating satire on the moral and financial corruption of a fast-growing commercial society and in particular the corruption of Sir Robert Walpole's government. Witty and fast-moving, its characters have become household names. Through the eternal triangle of Polly Peachum, the innocent but feisty heroine, Lucy Lockit, her wronged rival, and Macheath, their unreliable, irrepressible highwayman lover, Gay explores the pleasures and dangers of romantic and social aspiration. And in the figure of Peachum, the double-dealing thief-taker, he embodies the ruthless self-interest of his age and the fine line between respectability and criminality. A skilled mixture of genres and influences, the play is steeped in literary tradition and is at the same time an example of eighteenth-century popular culture at its best. Its entertaining, uncompromising exposure of corruption makes it equally a drama for the twenty-first century.

Summary of the Plot

Polly Peachum, daughter of a fence and thief-taker, has secretly married Macheath, a notorious highwayman. Horrified at their daughter throwing herself away on such a man, Mr and Mrs Peachum plot to extricate Polly from the marriage, as well as to profit from it, by turning in their son-in-law, collecting the reward for doing so, and seeing him hanged. The besotted Polly helps Macheath escape, but he is betrayed by a group of whores in Peachum's pay and taken to Newgate prison where he is once

---

1 No fewer than 13 adaptations made since 1928 are listed in Uwe Böker et al. eds., *John Gay's The Beggar's Opera 1728–2004: Adaptations and Re-Writings*, 2004, pp. 7–8.

again helped to escape by Lucy Lockit, daughter of the prison-keeper, who is pregnant by him and to whom he has also promised marriage. While Polly and Lucy fight over Macheath, with Lucy trying to poison Polly, Lockit and Peachum conspire and succeed in having him again captured and imprisoned. Polly and Lucy plead for his life, as do four more women maintaining that he has married them and is father of their children. Claiming to prefer the gallows, he is nevertheless saved from hanging by a last-minute reprieve.

The Play

The Beggar's Opera is one of a number of hugely popular, ground-breaking works which reflected early eighteenth-century London back to itself. Through their experiments with form across a variety of genres, *The Beggar's Opera*, Daniel Defoe's novel *Moll Flanders* (1722), and William Hogarth's narrative print series *A Harlot's Progress* (1732), engaged with the complexities of city life and catered for a new, mixed, urban audience. The reflection they offer to their 'respectable' audiences and readers is unflattering – but still powerfully recognisable. What they have in common – other than their innovative, experimental quality – is a fascination with 'low life' and criminality. Through their focus on London's underworld, they expose the moral, social and political tensions and uncertainties which were engendered at all levels of society as rapid commercial expansion created opportunity, nurtured corruption and reinforced inequality. As a result, the protagonists of these works transcended their immediate context to take on the status of cultural myths. Like Defoe's Moll Flanders and Hogarth's harlot, Gay's Peachum, Polly and Macheath seized the popular imagination as the embodiments of a culture in which the lines between respectability and criminality, purity and corruption, were dangerously – or, perhaps, excitingly – blurred.

The Ballad Opera: Gay's experiments with genre

Gay announces these social ambivalences in the very title of his play. Audiences at the Theatre Royal in Lincoln's Inn Fields where *The Beggar's Opera* opened on 29 January 1728 would have been intrigued by the contradictory suggestion that beggars might have anything to do with opera, a genre concerned in its subject-matter with gods and heroes, honour and romance. In the early eighteenth century opera-going was a comparatively new and fashionable pastime. It was a sign of wealth and, supposedly, of refined taste; it was also identified with a taste for things foreign, since the style of opera dominant at the time derived from Italy. Gay's new genre – the ballad opera – knowingly challenges each of these associations and, in doing so, makes clear its satirical intent as well as its appeal to a wider audience. Set in the present, in and around Newgate prison, it replaces gods and heroes with thief-catchers, criminals and prostitutes; it draws on popular, indigenous culture, using ballad tunes which would have been familiar to audiences from across the social spectrum; and it presents a world where honour and romance are fatally tainted by corruption and self-interest.

Though 'ballad opera' is the way it is usually defined, *The Beggar's Opera* defies any easy generic categorisation. As Margaret Doody has suggested, 'It imitates nothing, though it borrows from almost everything; it is definitely, almost defiantly *sui generis*'.[2] These 'borrowings', the ingredients of Gay's generic mix, include opera itself; neo-classical satiric poetry; Restoration and sentimental comedy; broadside ballads and satires; and criminal narratives – a range which also reflects the tastes of audiences at every social level.

Gay's drama establishes its generic daring and subtlety from the beginning, in the introductory encounter between the Beggar and the Player. Their brief interchange emphasises the primacy of aesthetic quality over social status, insisting that 'poetical merit' transcends the superficialities of rank. The Muses, we are told, 'pay no distinction to dress', distinguishing instead between true wit and the mere 'embroidery' of style. The appeal, typical of Gay and his circle, is to a discerning taste uninhibited by the rules of fashion or genre. In this inclusive and discriminating context, the Beggar can assert that his work 'must be allowed [to be] an opera in all its forms', in spite of its having been written not for contemporary opera stars but for the marriage of 'two most excellent ballad singers' – street entertainers often associated with criminality – and in spite of the fact that it deals in reality and is not 'throughout unnatural, like those in vogue' (Introduction, 6-24).

Since its first appearance in the 1705-06 season, the style of opera 'in vogue' on the London stage was Italian, not British. Rather than mixing reflective arias with spoken dialogue, Italian opera was sung throughout, its dialogue and action conducted through recitative, a style of delivery half way between melody and speech. It was this, together with the elaborate and often spectacular staging – not to mention the importance of the *castrato* voice and the celebrity of the *castrati* singers in polite society – which led its critics to dismiss it as 'unnatural'. In 1723, a few years before he wrote *The Beggar's Opera*, Gay commented on this fashionable cultural obsession in a letter to Jonathan Swift:

---

2 Margaret Doody, *The Daring Muse: Augustan Poetry Reconsidered*, 1985, p. 212.

As for the reigning Amusement of the town, tis entirely Musick. …
Theres nobody allow'd to say I sing but an Eunuch or an Italian
Woman. Every body is grown now as great a judge of Musick
as they were in your time of Poetry. and folks that could not
distinguish one tune from another now daily dispute about the
different Styles of Hendel, Bononcini, and Attillio. People have
now forgot Homer, and Virgil & Caesar, or at least they have lost
their ranks, for in London and Westminster in all polite
conversation's Senesino is daily voted to be the greatest man that
ever liv'd.[3]

It would be a mistake, however, to assume that The Beggar's Opera is
either simply an attack on Italian opera or, as some critics have argued, a
straightforward defence of a British operatic tradition. Swift's typically
uncompromising judgement was that Gay's drama 'exposeth with Great
Justice that unnatural Taste for Italian Musick among us, which is wholly
unsuitable to our Northern Climate, and the Genius of the People,
whereby we are overrun with Italian-Effeminacy, and Italian Nonsense'.[4]
This has sometimes been simplistically read as authoritative evidence that
Gay hated Italian opera, used The Beggar's Opera to ridicule it, and
intended his work as a defence of the British tradition. But with characteristic sophistication, Gay's drama draws on both traditions in order to
create something very different. Like Italian opera, The Beggar's Opera has
three acts rather than the five usual in British examples, but it also reverts
in significant ways to a British form of musical drama, or 'semi-opera'.
Most notably, it does not use recitative, and it does not indulge in spec-
tacle. But it is also innovative, taking its 'Britishness' much further into
the realm of popular culture than any of its predecessors, both in its subject-matter and in its use of popular airs and ballad tunes. In a telling
departure from the heroic or tragic modes which dominated the Italian
and the British operatic traditions, it is a 'low' comedy. The 'ballad opera'
which results is a complex form of burlesque in which the mock-heroic
imitation of operatic conventions invites satirical reflection not so much
on opera itself as on the society which allowed its excesses to become 'the

---

3 [sic], The Letters of John Gay, ed. C. F. Burgess, 1966, p. 43. There was intense rivalry between George Frideric Handel (1685–1759) and the Italian composers Giovanni Bononcini
(1670–?1747) and Attilio Ariosti (1666–?1729), all members of the Royal Academy of
Music in London during the 1720s and composers of operas for the London stage;
Francesco Bernardi Senesino (1686–?1758), a celebrated castrato singer, was resident in
London during the 1720s and 30s.
4 The Intelligencer 3 (?25 May 1728); Jonathan Swift and Thomas Sheridan, The Intelligencer, ed. James Woolley, 1992, p. 65.

reigning Amusement of the town': a society where conspicuous consumption was underwritten by corruption, both symptom and cause of a shift to recognisably modern methods of financial (mis)management.

Though the genre of ballad opera was new, its satiric conjunction of high art with urban low life would have struck a more familiar chord with contemporary audiences. In *The Beggar's Opera*, Gay transfers to music-drama techniques from the poetry of the time, including his own. A key feature of the most interesting early-eighteenth-century poetry is the way in which it adapts classical forms in its effort to engage directly with modern subject matter, a mode associated particularly with the legacy of the Scriblerus Club. Together with Swift, Alexander Pope and others, Gay had been a member of this short-lived but highly influential grouping which came together in 1714 with the aim, according to Pope, 'to have ridiculed all the false tastes in learning'.[5] Satire was the Scriblerians' dominant mode as they defended traditional, classical standards of taste against the forces of modernity, or what Pope in his mock-epic *The Dunciad* dubbed 'Dullness'. Gay's letter to Swift quoted above, with its swipes at ignorant audiences and at the whims of a fashionable taste which preferred Italian opera stars to 'Homer, and Virgil & Caesar', is typical of the Scriblerian position. But, paradoxically, though their motivation was essentially conservative, the Scriblerians produced some of the most innovative and entertaining poetry of this or any other period. The mixture of revulsion and fascination with which Gay, Swift and Pope responded to contemporary literary and political culture finds expression in their experiments in mock-heroic and, most interestingly from the point of view of *The Beggar's Opera*, in mock-georgic, in which they applied the conventions of pastoral poetry, with its celebration of a simple rural existence and rural labour, to the very different life of the city.

In 1716 Swift famously asked Pope, 'what think you of a Newgate pastoral, among the whores and thieves there?', and he thought that 'our friend Gay' would be the writer best fitted to take on this unlikely project.[6] Whether Gay ever heard of this plan is unknown. But even if there is no direct connection with *The Beggar's Opera*, Swift's suggestion usefully illustrates the kinds of projects which excited the Scriblerian imagination and which are still very much in evidence in Gay's drama.

---

5 Joseph Spence, *Anecdotes*, Section I 1728–30, quoted in Charles Kerby-Miller, ed., *Memoirs of the Extraordinary Life, Works, and Discoveries of Martinus Scriblerus*, 1950, p. 363.

6 30 August 1716, *The Correspondence of Jonathan Swift*, ed. Harold Williams, 5 vols, 1963–5, II, 215.

Swift's comment also acknowledges Gay's particular skill in playing with genres to satiric effect. In January 1716, Gay had published *Trivia: Or, the Art of Walking the Streets of London*, a poem in three books based on the *Georgics* by the Latin poet Virgil. Like the relationship between *The Beggar's Opera*, which is about 'whores and thieves', and conventional opera, which is about heroes, the relationship between *Trivia*, which guides the reader through the bustle, squalor and suffering of London, and the *Georgics*, which are about farming, is one of comic incongruity. But it is serious comedy. *Trivia* celebrates London's multifariousness; it also stresses the moral superiority of the poet who walks through the city in company with labourers, street-vendors and the poor, over the man rich enough to travel by coach and thus able to ignore the fact that 'The starving orphan, as he passes, weeps' (*Trivia*, Book II, 580). Far from invoking classical forms simply in order to criticise an inadequate present, Gay expands their subject-matter, turning Virgil's study of rural labour into a strikingly democratic reminder of the forms of work which support London's rich and powerful by day and of the criminal street life which gives the city a grotesque energy by night.

The relationship between Gay's 'Newgate pastoral' and its operatic and classical antecedents carries the same ambivalent energy. The protagonists are criminals and double-dealers, and to that extent represent a failure of heroic ideals; their 'work' is crime, and to that extent represents the loss of honest pastoral labour. As the Beggar's moralising summary at the end very clearly puts it, 'the whole piece' has demonstrated 'such a similitude of manners in high and low life, that it is difficult to determine whether, in the fashionable vices, the fine gentlemen imitate the gentlemen of the road, or the gentlemen of the road, the fine gentlemen' (III.xvi.15-19). At one level, then, Gay's generic experiment in mock-heroic, mock-pastoral drama is a general satire on the whole of society, dismissing respectable and criminal classes alike. But Gay's generic borrowings have a more complex moral effect. Like the people of the streets who are given status and significance in *Trivia*, Gay's criminal protagonists are far more than simply a means of attacking those in power, and more than merely objects of vilification themselves: they also excite our sympathy.

This complexity of response has much to do with Gay's readiness to borrow from non-classical and popular cultural genres rather than just those associated with a more educated social elite. The most obvious examples are his use of traditional song tunes, familiar to audiences from all social backgrounds, his play with the conventions of early eighteenth-century comedy, often seen as a particularly middle-class form of entertainment, and his awareness of popular criminal narratives. Some of

Gay's chosen airs evoke a quality of feeling or a lost pastoral world which are often disturbingly at odds with the song's immediate context in the play. The effect is to lend whichever character sings the air a complex emotional individuality which plays on the audience's sympathies. At such moments, *The Beggar's Opera* takes on the feel of a sentimental comedy, the most successful example of which in the 1720s was Richard Steele's *The Conscious Lovers* (1722). More concerned with pathos than humour, sentimental comedy defined itself against the brittle aristocratic cynicism of Restoration comedy, focusing typically on a virtuous couple of the middling sort who survive a variety of moral trials and are rewarded with domestic bliss. This is the genre which helps shape Polly's aspirations, in which she most readily imagines herself taking a starring role. Sadly for her, however, Macheath comes from the earlier genre; he is a lower-class parody of a Restoration rake such as Dorimant, the amoral and unreliable protagonist in George Etherege's *The Man of Mode* (1676) who, like Macheath, plays unrepentantly with the affections of several women.

Macheath's other main generic antecedent is the 'rogue narrative'. The life-stories of notorious criminals, particularly highwaymen and prostitutes, were a particularly successful popular cultural form. Claiming a usually spurious authenticity and sometimes presented as confessional testimonies before execution, such narratives satisfied a public fascinated by criminality, but also by the often fine line between criminality and financial and social success. Some of these narratives appeared as broadsides, cheap single-sheet publications; at their most sophisticated, they lie behind Defoe's novels *Moll Flanders* and *Colonel Jack* (both 1722) in which the protagonists are characterised by their capacity to survive and succeed, through a mixture of 'respectable' and criminal means, in a predatory world. Colonel Jack is by turns soldier, thief, plantation owner, trader, pirate and smuggler. Moll is a wife, prostitute and thief; Jemmy, her favourite among her five husbands, is a highwayman. Reunited during transportation to the American colonies, Moll and Jemmy become rich plantation owners. Defoe's fiction, like Gay's drama, brings out the tension already inherent in rogue narratives between the impulse to celebrate the criminals' daring as a kind of popular heroism and the moral imperative to condemn them as the sign of a more general corruption. The resourcefulness of the highwayman, robbing the coaches of the rich, or of the prostitute, exploiting men's sexual weaknesses, is seen to mirror the no less ruthless means to social and financial success which were accepted as legitimate in a world of rapid commercial expansion. In Gay's play, Macheath is very obviously the romantic, brutal highwayman; Jenny

Diver, the canny prostitute. More specifically, behind Gay's Peachum, in cahoots with both criminals and the law, lies the real-life figure of the notorious thief-catcher and receiver of stolen goods, Jonathan Wild, whose trial and execution in 1725 spawned an industry of popular publications.

Gay's ballad opera ran for a record sixty-two performances after its opening in January 1728 and its popularity extended through spin-off publications and artefacts, both written and visual, to audiences well beyond those able to afford the cost of a theatre ticket or even to read. Gay had created a new genre, but it was his sophisticated borrowings from other genres at all levels of 1720s culture that gave his ballad opera its universal appeal – as entertainment, as a complex portrait of characters from the lower rungs of society, and as political and social satire.

Satire, Structure and Language

The play's opening scenes deftly set up its satiric mode, establish its governing themes and preoccupations, and familiarise the audience with the balance of song and dialogue through which its meanings are structured. *The Beggar's Opera* announces itself as a general satire on corruption from its opening song. The original lyrics of 'An Old Woman Clothed in Gray' told the oft-repeated tale of the seduction of a trusting young woman. In Gay's version, sung by the fence and thief-taker Peachum, abuse of trust infects every personal and professional relationship, from family and neighbours up to the statesman who 'Thinks his trade as honest as mine' (I.i.8). The audience is left to judge whether the statesman's assumption is a matter of naivety, disingenu-ousness or unashamed dishonesty. Peachum's dishonesty, and that of the legal system he exploits and supports, are left in no doubt, however, as he proudly announces his self-interested 'double capacity, both against rogues and for 'em' (I.i.10). He is both protector to and informant on the criminal gang which, like an early-eighteenth-century godfather, he controls through a mixture of incentives and threats. Whether, and how, Peachum might himself be outwitted, how the comparison with 'the statesman' might be demonstrated, and whether the society Peachum represents can be redeemed, become structuring questions in the drama.

From the opening scenes, then, Peachum, whose name means to inform against or betray, becomes the embodiment of a society governed by self-interest and double-dealing: a figure we love to hate, and long to see toppled. For a contemporary audience, his status as the representative of endemic corruption was further reinforced through the obvious identification of Peachum with the real-life figure of Jonathan Wild, the notorious 'Thief-catcher General'. In the 1710s and 1720s, initially through collaboration with a corrupt City Marshal, Wild both ran the London underworld and brought about the arrest and conviction of large numbers of criminals at a time when official law enforcement was strikingly ineffectual. Like Peachum, Wild encouraged criminals to inform against each other, thus gaining control of the gangs; and, like Peachum, he acted as both commissioner and fence for stolen goods. Indeed, in Wild's case, he fronted his criminal involvement by running an 'Office of Intelligence for lost Goods', a shady public service which, for a pre-agreed fee, restored to their owners goods which had been stolen on Wild's orders. Wild's methods were widely known but difficult to prove – particularly by collusive officers of the law. His daring and his genius as a self-publicist earned him some public sympathy, until in 1724 he engineered the conviction of Jack Sheppard, one of the most notorious criminals of the day and one of the figures invoked by Gay's Macheath. Sheppard had succeeded in maintaining his independence of Wild, as a result of which the popular press took Sheppard's side, representing him as the principled underdog (comparatively speaking), and public opinion turned against the thief-catcher. When Wild eventually became careless and was convicted in 1725 of receiving a reward for goods he knew to be stolen, a huge crowd turned out to celebrate his hanging.

Sensationalist and burlesque narratives of Wild's career abounded after his death, but Gay was the first to suggest a satiric analogy between Wild and the most powerful political figure of the day Sir Robert Walpole, first minister and leader of the parliamentary Whigs.[7] Walpole was already the frequent object of Tory satire, and a contemporary audience would have immediately picked up this specifically political agenda from that pointed comparison in the opening song between Peachum and 'the statesman'. Jibes against Walpole recur throughout *The Beggar's Opera*. At times it is Peachum, with his 'double capacity', who appears to represent the first minister; at others, Walpole's political daring seems closer to aspects of Macheath's ability to extricate himself from seemingly impossible situations; at others again, he is reduced to a member of the gang, 'Robin of Bagshot, alias Gorgon, alias Bob Bluff, alias Carbuncle, alias Bob Booty' (I.iii.27-8), a common thief at the mercy either of Peachum or, in an allusion to the widely-known fact that Walpole kept a mistress, of the prostitutes he cannot resist. As Peachum tells his wife in the opening scenes, no doubt to knowing laughter from a contemporary audience, 'I have set his name down in the black list, that's all, my dear; he spends his life among women, and as soon as all his

---

7 Walpole was not generally known as 'Prime Minister', a role he created, until the early 1730s.

money is gone, one or other of the ladies will hang him for the reward' (I.iv.4-6). Peachum's boasted power over Bob Booty plays on contemporary fantasies of seeing 'the great man', as Walpole was known, brought low, just as Jonathan Wild had been.

Gay and his Scriblerian literary associates were out of sympathy with the court of George I, which favoured Walpole and the Whigs, and Gay had bitter experience of failing to attract the court patronage which would have secured him a salaried post. As Chancellor of the Exchequer and First Lord of the Treasury, Walpole had been identified (not entirely fairly) with the uncontrolled financial speculation and then the spectacular failure in 1722 of what became known as the South Sea Bubble – in effect, the first stock market crash – in which Gay himself lost a considerable amount of money. A skilled and persuasive manager of government and parliament and an astute political survivor, Walpole stood in the popular satirical imagination for dubious financial methods and unscrupulous power-seeking by means of bribery and patronage. At the time Gay was writing The Beggar's Opera, these qualities had been brought into even sharper focus. Following the death of George I in June 1727, Walpole unexpectedly survived the jostling for political influence which accompanied George II's accession to the throne. Largely, it was thought, through his influence over Queen Caroline and the mobilisation of rumours of a likely Jacobite uprising, Walpole succeeded in consolidating not just the protestant Hanoverian succession but also his own power, establishing what his opponents, with grudging admiration, labelled 'the Robinocracy'.

These immediate contemporary contexts and public figures are a significant aspect of The Beggar's Opera. But the play is very far from being simply political allegory. Like the various characters who represent him, Walpole, the arch-survivor, himself becomes just another symptom of the much broader moral malaise exposed by the play. The choices it offers are, in the main, choices between villains, or between degrees of self-interest. In an environment where everyone has the power to 'peach' everyone else, and death or transportation is pretty much inevitable, the drama hangs on who will survive, how, and at what cost. At the level of narrative structure, it is survival – more specifically, the survival of Macheath – which shapes the play's three acts, each of which ends with his escape. And at the level of the individual scene, survival motivates the characters' attempts to outmanoeuvre each other, with the audience led to admire those who are most effective in outwitting their rivals.

Though The Beggar's Opera is about street-crime, the action of the play takes place indoors and its central narrative is a love story; and though the characters are criminals, they speak in the idiom of polite society. Gay uses the conventions of sentimental comedy to interrogate the gap between ideals and actuality in the increasingly consumerist economy of the 1720s, where personal wealth and upward social mobility were real possibilities. Significantly, the play begins in a domestic interior, Peachum's house, with Peachum '*sitting at a table with a large book of accounts before him*' (I.i.0), the image of the businessman at home. It becomes immediately clear, of course, that his business is hardly the 'honest employment' he claims (I.i.9), and the effect of these opening scenes is to raise uncomfortable questions about where the boundaries might lie between the underworld he inhabits and the value systems of the respectable world of the middling, commercial and professional classes who made up a good proportion of the audience. The goods he receives are the fashionable goods they trade, or buy, or aspire to own; he claims to be as 'honest' as any lawyer, a comparison guaranteed to invoke hollow laughter; his wife mimics the pastimes of society with her planned 'party of quadrille', for example (I.iv.42-3); and, most tellingly, his daughter Polly aspires 'to make the most of myself and of my man too', in the manner of 'fine ladies' (I.vii.1-2).

Gay's domestic setting and love plot demonstrate the intimate connection between the private, domestic sphere of emotional attachment and personal loyalties, and the public world of money-getting. Peachum's claim to 'honest employment' holds up a revealing mirror to the public world of sanctioned commercial exchange, where greed and self-interest are thinly disguised by the rules of social politeness and business protocols. At the same time, when Mrs Peachum invokes the 'honour of our family' (I.vi.36), and insists that Polly's 'duty' to her parents means betraying her husband to the hangman, the mirror is turned on the private world of domestic relationships and values. The Peachum parents can't afford, or risk, the kind of sentiment which Polly claims to represent. For them, family values have been irreparably corrupted by the need to survive, a point very obviously made through the darkly comic gap between their use of the moral language of 'honour' and 'duty' and their cynical assumption that marriage is a mercenary power struggle.

This gap between the world the characters inhabit and the language of social ideals and moral respectability which they speak is maintained as we are introduced to Polly's lover, Macheath, and the members of his gang. Act Two opens in the semi-public interior of '*a tavern near Newgate*' (II.i.0) as the play changes focus from the family to a rather different social group: the gang. Like the Peachums, this dominantly masculine community also claims to live according to codes of 'honour' and 'duty', conducting highway robbery on principles of 'conduct and discretion' (II.ii.25). But Macheath and his gang also declare themselves to be 'gentlemen of the sword' (II.iii.6) and invoke a masculine honour code based on the 'the law of arms and the right of conquest' (II.i.10-11). This extends the play's satirical reach up the social hierarchy. It identifies Macheath not as an aspirant member of the respectable bourgeoisie, like Polly, but as a parody of the aristocratic libertine figure whose conquests are largely sexual – an identity made very clear in his self-justifying soliloquy about the impossibility of being satisfied by one woman (II.iii.1-7).

Macheath's men have names that might be drawn from one of the popular slang dictionaries of the time, offering Gay's respectable audience the thrill of vicarious access to the criminal underworld by way of its distinctive jargon.[8] But the criminals themselves speak the language of polite society. They euphemistically enjoy the prospect of 'taking the air' as they plan highway robbery on Hounslow Heath, for example (II.ii.5); and when he is first imprisoned, Macheath negotiates with Lockit for the most comfortable fetters as if he were a man of fashion choosing a pair of boots (II.vii.3-11). The distance, but also the uncomfortable similarities, between the criminals and the theatre audience are comically reinforced through these witty and unexpected uses of a shared idiom of politeness; and such language complicates the ways in which we judge the characters and their activities.

The other language at work in *The Beggar's Opera* is of course the language of music. The songs change the pace of the drama, providing moments of reflection; and by drawing on well-known tunes, they introduce a wider context which further complicates the satirical nature and messages of the play. Sometimes the effect is simply to reinforce the play's unremitting depiction of corrupt self-interest – as in Peachum's opening song, 'Through all the employments of life', for example (I.i.1). More often, however, the situation or emotion articulated in Gay's lyrics is complicated by the different kinds of associations evoked by the tune. Air 16 (I.xiii.30), for example, is a song of love and longing as Polly and Macheath face the prospect of separation, but the tune, 'Over the hills and far away', had been widely used in songs on political issues ranging from the Jacobite cause to the South Sea Bubble. The effect is to critique the longing for escape articulated in Gay's lyrics: private relationships, it is suggested, can never break free of wider public events. And throughout the play, there is frequently a complex structural irony in the relationship between the

---

8 Just one example is *A New Canting Dictionary: Comprehending All the Terms, Antient and Modern, used in the Several Tribes of Gypsies, Beggars, Shoplifters, Highwaymen, Foot Pads, and all other Clans of Cheats and Villains*, 1725, used in the commentary on the text.

songs and the characters who sing them. Thieves and prostitutes give voice to exquisite pastoral lyrics; the tawdry libertine Macheath sings of undying love; Polly and Lucy share duets which transcend their bitter rivalry for Macheath's affections. The negative reading of these ironic contrasts is to point out the characters' failure to live up to the sentiments expressed in the songs. This is valid, but too simple. The power of the music lends power to the sentiments themselves so that the songs function as poignant reminders – for the characters as well as the audience – of a more innocent world. The challenge for anyone staging Gay's complex play is to find ways of capturing this delicate balance of satire and sentiment.

Characters

In William Hogarth's narrative print series, *A Harlot's Progress* (1732), a portrait of 'Captain Macheath' decorates the harlot's sordid lodgings in Drury Lane. The detail is a reminder of the strong thematic connection between Gay's play and Hogarth's visual moral satire, as well as a subtle tribute to the close professional link between Gay and Hogarth, who had produced a series of paintings of a scene from *The Beggar's Opera*. But the harlot's intertextual pin-up also provides a touch of authenticity. Hundreds of cheap print portraits of Thomas Walker, who played Macheath in the first production, were sold at the time and must have decorated many comparatively humble rooms in London and beyond. Even more popular were pictures and mementos featuring the eighteen-year-old Lavinia Fenton, the first Polly, whose celebrity status was further enhanced when she left the production just before the end of the run to elope with the Duke of Bolton.

As well as making celebrities of the leading actors, the huge success of Gay's play ensured that its main characters – Polly and Macheath – entered the realm of cultural myth. Helped by Lavinia Fenton's interpretation of the role, Polly Peachum came to represent the precarious survival of innocence and loyalty in the midst of corruption. The first-night audience was said to be won over by Fenton's moving rendition of Polly's song 'Oh ponder well' (Air 12; I.x.40-3), and following the publication of prints of Polly/Fenton, Gay reported to Swift that 'I am in doubt, whether her fame does not surpass that of the Opera itself'.[9] Similarly, in the popular imagination the name of the fictional Macheath was added to those of Robin Hood and, later, Dick Turpin – legendary outlaw heroes celebrated because their criminal exploits became identified with natural justice. It's an identity self-consciously invoked by Macheath and his men

9 *Letters of John Gay*, p. 73.

in the play: as Ben Budge puts it, 'We are for a just partition of the world, for every man hath a right to enjoy life' (II.i.19-20). The validity of such claims is for readers, directors and audiences to decide.

How we interpret Gay's play, and what version of society we think it endorses, rests above all on how we judge Polly and Macheath. Peachum, Mrs Peachum and Lockit are comic villains, irredeemably corrupt; the pregnant Lucy, abused by Macheath but ready to poison Polly in order to save herself, has become corrupted, a fallen woman in all senses. To this extent, the play presents an amoral world governed by survival, self-interest and duplicity – Peachum's 'double capacity' (I.i.10). In contemporary minds, such a world-view would be associated with the philosopher Thomas Hobbes in his *Leviathan* (1651) for whom, famously, human life in its natural state is 'nasty, brutish and short' and society is a necessary form of 'protection and defence' against the potentially destructive self-interest of individuals or, as Hobbes puts it, 'such a war as is of every man against every man'.[10] But the figures of Macheath and especially Polly demand a more complicated judgement, as their contemporary popularity suggests. For the modern audience, particularly, that judgement will depend very much on how we view the play's sexual politics. To what extent are we prepared to credit Macheath's representation of himself in terms of honour and generosity, a flawed but dashing form of masculinity which in the world of the play is at least preferable to the deeper villainy of his captors? And how far are we convinced by Polly's version of herself as wronged, innocent femininity, the stereotypical victim of sentimental narrative who clings in spite of all to her ideal of faithful love? Like the songs Polly and Macheath sing, such characterisations offer a tantalising glimpse of an alternative philosophy, associated in contemporary terms with the work of Anthony Ashley Cooper, third Earl of Shaftesbury, whose *Characteristicks of Men, Manners, Opinions, Times* (1711) sees humanity as inherently sociable and capable of virtuous action, selflessness and solidarity. One question at the heart of *The Beggar's Opera* is whether and how such a belief, and those that hold it, can survive in Peachum's world.

In an environment in which survival is paramount, the focus falls on what makes an individual vulnerable to betrayal and how successfully they manage that vulnerability. In the case of Macheath, his chances of ending up on the gallows – as well as the possibility of escape – are defined as much by his penchant for women as by his criminal activities. His addiction to sexual pleasure is an inextricable feature of the libertine

---

10 Thomas Hobbes, *Leviathan* (1651), 'Introduction' and Chap. XIII.

heroism on which he models himself: 'I must have women', he announces, offering by way of justification the rake's brutally self-serving argument that by indulging his personal pleasures he helps keep London supplied with prostitutes (II.iii.19, 3-7). Macheath is something of a caricatured highwayman-hero, given to impressing Polly through parodic and self-evidently unreliable protestations of love: 'May my pistols misfire, and my mare slip her shoulder while I am pursued, if I ever forsake thee!' (I.xiii.13-14). Nevertheless, for the play to work, the audience must be convinced of his sexual attractiveness. Less straightforward is how the play invites us to judge its consequences for Polly, Lucy, the group of prostitutes in Act Two and, at the very end, four 'women more . . . with a child apiece' (III.xv.21), all of whom Macheath has used and betrayed. How we react to Macheath's final reprieve will depend very much on the extent to which we are prepared to tolerate his sexual self-indulgence.

As with everything else in Gay's text, there is no simple answer. At one level, the play is alert to the way in which men like Macheath are responsible for making women peculiarly vulnerable. According to the sexual double standard which prevailed at the time, promiscuous masculinity was condoned, or even admired, whilst sexually active women were condemned as whores. This is Lucy's plight: having been unfortunate, or foolish, enough to become pregnant she is 'forced to bear about the load of infamy' (II.ix.3). Lucy is an object of pity and some of her songs, particularly her duets with Polly, enlist our sympathy. But she is ultimately too much of a victim and her vengeful naivety is too out of control for her to be the heroine.

Polly, by contrast, is both cannier and more idealistic than Lucy and a better match for Macheath – though precisely how canny and how idealistic is again a matter for individual actors, directors and readers to decide. As befits the daughter of the Peachums, she ensures her own survival within the terms dictated by the double standard, exploiting Macheath's desire and using her body as a bargaining counter, trading 'trifling liberties' for 'visible marks of his favour' (I.vii.5-6). But where she differs from her parents is in her claim to have married Macheath for love; and where she becomes most vulnerable is in her apparent belief that he is capable of reciprocating her love in her own monogamous terms. Smart enough to anticipate Lucy's attempts to poison her, it is Polly's emotional, rather than her physical survival which is in danger.

The fact that Polly's family and the object of her affections are rather less than respectable only makes her social and emotional aspirations all the more precarious – or, to put it more harshly, ridiculous. And in believing that she can tame the libertine into a respectable marriage, Polly falls for an eighteenth-century cliché. The moral advice literature of the time constantly warned young women against any such expectation. It is here that Polly's identification with the bourgeois family values of sentimental comedy is most clearly at odds with Macheath's Restoration masculinity. But Polly and Macheath are nevertheless well matched, equally capable of turning this clash of values to their own advantage. Polly plays on Macheath's aspirations to heroism when she reminds him, for example, that in the romance that he lent her 'none of the great heroes were ever false in love' (I.xiii.16-17); he in turn draws attention to her misplaced social ambitions and ridicules the way in which, 'like other fine ladies', she assumes a man could be 'her own for ever and ever' (II.ix.54–5). Individual productions must decide how far they want to endorse Macheath's version of things and suggest that Polly, Lucy and their romantic aspirations are absurdly inappropriate. But Macheath's sexual appetite reduces him, too, to absurdity. Confronted by both Polly and Lucy – and later four other wives – Macheath, the libertine wannabe, is ultimately himself an outdated figure of fun.

There is one character, however, who successfully escapes the sexual power play and the vulnerability it brings. Like Moll Flanders in Defoe's novel, Jenny Diver is the play's survivor (and she reappears in Gay's sequel, *Polly*, which follows the characters to the West Indies after Macheath's transportation). Disappointed once by Macheath, she has developed 'a command of the passions uncommon in a woman' and knows better than to mix business with pleasure: 'I have other hours, and other sort of men for my pleasure' (II.iv.69, 71). Hardened by experience, it is Jenny who turns Macheath over to Peachum and the constables in the second act, and her two songs (Airs 23 and 24) are cynical commentaries on male power and on a society run according to the values of 'gamesters and lawyers' (II.iv.110).

In one way, then, Jenny Diver might be seen as the satirical voice of the play. But Gay's deceptively complex text is most interested in those characters who find themselves caught between what they desire and what they can get, what they can imagine and what they can achieve. It's a tension which is at the heart of all satire, where the impulse to rail against things as they are is born of disappointment that things are not as they might be. In *The Beggar's Opera*, this ambivalence is most powerfully captured through the distorted romance of Macheath and Polly Peachum, and through Gay's innovative juxtaposition of spoken drama and music where satiric laughter is frequently qualified by pathos. The airs sung by Gay's whores and highwaymen, and particularly by Polly and Macheath, offer a precarious alternative to self-interest and double-dealing by giving a fleeting immediacy to feelings of love and longing. By shamelessly playing on the audience's capacity for sentiment in this way, the play makes clear what is lost when financial and political corruption and the will to survive are a society's dominant characteristics.

The Beggar's Opera in the eighteenth-century theatre

The Theatre Royal, Lincoln's Inn Fields, where *The Beggar's Opera* opened, had been rebuilt by John Rich's father Christopher, in 1712.[11] It followed the standard 'three-space' design of the period: at the rear, and comparatively dimly lit, was the 'scene'. Here combinations of side wings and painted shutters were wheeled in and out on grooved tracks in the stage floor to represent stock scenes. Except on rare occasions these would not have been prepared for a particular play, and *The Beggar's Opera*'s tavern and prison settings would have been familiar to the original audience. The scenic demands of the first two acts are straightforward; only in the third is a scene required more than once, and it is likely that advantage was taken of the possibility of preparing one scene in the space behind another, so that the table and props specified in III.v, for example, might have been exposed as shutters parted, and then have been removed during the subsequent Newgate scene before the Condemned Hold was revealed as a finale. This final scene was probably set furthest back, in what would appropriately be the dimmest part of the stage; the stage direction implies that Macheath was 'discovered' in this space in his '*melancholy posture*'. He would, however, almost certainly have quickly moved forward, for action did not take place principally within a realistically imagined space defined by the scenery but on a thrust stage extending in front of the scene. A 'green curtain' divided scene and acting areas. It was raised at the play's opening, and probably remained open throughout. Perhaps the Introduction was played in front of this curtain, which then lifted at the end of the overture.

Actors customarily entered and left the acting area directly from side-doors rather than from the back through the scene. Polly and Macheath clearly leave by these doors in their affecting leave-taking at the end of I.xiii. This would have been the most brightly lit part of the theatre, with chandeliers overhead, lamps set at the front as footlights, and mirrors on the side walls to reflect the light. In front of the stage, where a row of spikes established a barrier, the small orchestra was placed; beyond was the audience in the pit. As well as galleries and boxes round the auditorium, the audience also occupied boxes extending onto the sides of

---

11 For a detailed account of the theatre see Paul Sawyer, *The New Theatre in Lincoln's Inn Fields*, 1979.

the acting area, and might even sit or stand on the stage itself. Hogarth's paintings of III.xi cannot be taken literally as representations of what the theatre audience saw,[12] but in two versions he accurately shows the audience crowding round the action. On at least one occasion no less than 98 persons occupied the stage area, in a total audience of over 1300.[13] The relationship between actors and audience was, then, potentially a close one. As in the Elizabethan theatre, it was easy for actors to speak directly to the audience, and this proximity undoubtedly also facilitated easy transition from spoken to sung material.

It has sometimes been asserted that Gay himself wanted his tunes sung without accompaniment, and that instruments were only added as a last-minute modification. This is inherently unlikely, yet it was essential to their original effect that the songs were very lightly accompanied, were only briefly prefaced by playing over the first phrase or two, and were probably concluded by a coda repeating the final phrase.[14] Instruments simply doubled the voices, with a harpsichord supplying the harmonic infilling. Jeremy Barlow's recording recreates this original sound, which is heard also in Jonathan Miller's television production of 1983.[15] The brevity of the songs was significantly part of their point – explicitly distancing them from the extended arias of Italian operas.

The Beggar's Opera was, however, rearranged in various ways during its eighteenth-century theatrical life. Originally written for actors who could sing, the parts were increasingly taken by some of the foremost singers of the time, whether or not they could act particularly well.[16] The music itself was adapted and re-scored, notably by Thomas Linley in 1777 for a version prepared by Sheridan (of which little survives), presaging the many later modifications and rearrangements of the score.[17] But alteration went, on occasion, further than that. In response to growing criticism of the morality of the ending a version was created in which Macheath was sentenced to 'heave ballast upon the river for three years'; in some performances, presumably further to defuse the accusation that the work was an incitement to vice, Macheath was played by a woman.[18]

12 On the paintings see David Bindman and Scott Wilcox, eds., *"Among the Whores and Thieves": William Hogarth and The Beggar's Opera*, 1997.
13 Calhoun Winton, *John Gay and the London Theatre*, 1993, p. 102.
14 See Jeremy Barlow, *The Music of the Beggar's Opera*, 1990, pp. ix–xi.
15 *The Beggar's Opera*, The Broadside Band, dir. Jeremy Barlow, Hyperion 1114634.
16 Roger Fiske, *English Theatre Music in the Eighteenth Century*, 2nd ed., 1986 pp. 102–3.
17 See Fiske, pp. 399–407, and Jeremy Barlow, 'Published Arrangements of *The Beggar's Opera*, 1729–1990, *The Musical Times*, 131 (1990), pp. 533–8.
18 See C. Price, ed., *The Dramatic Works of Richard Brinsley Sheridan*, 1973, vol. 2, p. 777; Fiske, *Theatre Music*, pp. 402–6.

In 1781 George Colman the elder mounted a burlesque production in which all parts were sex-reversed. These transformations signal that the work was losing its immediate satiric purchase and anticipate the modern turning of Gay's work into something of a theatrical romp. *The Beggar's Opera* was itself adapted in the anonymous *Bow-Street Opera* of 1773. Its title-page declares that it was 'written on the plan of The Beggar's Opera; all the most celebrated songs of which are parodied; and the whole piece adapted to modern times, manners, and characters', thus beginning the series of re-applications and re-writings that are such an important feature of the theatrical history of Gay's work.

The Beggar's Opera in the modern theatre

The popularity of *The Beggar's Opera* declined during the nineteenth century, and it was after a lapse of about fifty years that Nigel Playfair's 1920 production revived its fortunes. It took London by storm, racking up over 1450 consecutive performances. The script was adapted (and bowdlerised) by Arnold Bennett, the music arranged by Frederic Austin, omitting a third of the original airs, including, significantly and symptomatically, Macheath's bitter commentary on the workings of justice in Air 57. Though the scoring included period instruments, Austin claimed that he wanted 'to make the musical interest sufficiently sustained and vivid for present purposes'. The costuming was in early eighteenth-century style; a *Times* correspondent's impression of it was 'one of daintiness. Even the women of the town are dainty.'[19] This was, then, a sanitised, decorative production, tilting the balance firmly towards the sentimental.

Yet it was in part the success of this production which caused Bertolt Brecht and his collaborator Elisabeth Hauptmann to translate, and then transform, Gay's work into *The Threepenny Opera*, first performed in 1928 and filmed in a substantially further modified version in 1931. Though Brecht follows the outline of Gay's work, and on occasion sticks closely to its text, all his changes, including the transformation of Macheath into a gangster-businessman, are directed to a highly politicised representation of the duplicitous morality, as Brecht saw it, of the bourgeoisie. Rejecting sympathetic identification with its characters, the adaptation abandons the moral equivocation of the original. Perhaps the most complete departure from the original was in the music, a new score provided by Kurt Weill in the musical idiom of the 1920s in which only one of the original melodies was retained. These songs (of which 'Mac the Knife' is the most

19 A.W.B., *The Times*, 10 November 1920.

celebrated) are more extended than those of the original, and generally offer an explicit, moralising commentary on the action.

These two productions usefully highlight the challenges that face any modern director of Gay's work. How should the tension between satire and sentiment so crucial to its effect and effectiveness be negotiated? How can the historical distance of *The Beggar's Opera* be spanned for a modern audience? What should be done with music that was once instantly recognisable, but now speaks an unfamiliar language?

Brecht's answer – to go for a thoroughgoing adaptation – is one which many have followed, including Vaclav Havel (*Zebrácká Opera*, 1975, in which there is no music) and Wole Soyinka (*Opera Wonyosi*, 1977), whose works commented savagely on political corruption in Czechoslovakia and Nigeria respectively. Others have spliced Gay's work into a different environment. Alan Ayckbourn's *A Chorus of Disapproval* (1994), for example, counterpoints the lives of a group of amateur actors with their rehearsal of a production of Gay's work, and Stephen Jeffreys in *The Convict's Opera* (2008/9) has Gay's opera being rehearsed on a convict ship bound for Australia.[20] But Brecht's work is also important to the recent theatre history of *The Beggar's Opera* itself, as Ned Chaillet observes:

> There are two fashions that seem to swamp the frequent revivals of *The Beggar's Opera*. Most recently it has been the desire to incorporate the play into the operatic repertoire, with full orchestrations and fuller voices. On the other side, many theatre directors seem to be listening in their hearts to *The Threepenny Opera*.[21]

The most complete 'operatisation' of Gay's work was undertaken in Benjamin Britten's frequently revived 1948 version. Britten retained most of the tunes, but extended many of them, creating duets and elaborate choruses, and transposing music to give a tonal consistency to the work as a whole. He felt that previous arrangements had avoided the airs' 'toughness and strangeness, and concentrated only on their lyrical prettiness', a danger his often astringent harmonisations avoided. But the elaboration of the music and abbreviation of the dialogue inevitably privileged the emotional plight of the central figures over more general satire.[22]

That it is possible entirely to anaesthetise *The Beggar's Opera*'s social commentary is amply demonstrated in the 1953 film, directed by Peter

---

20 See also Uwe Böker et al., eds., *John Gay's Beggar's Opera 1728–2004*, 2006, a collection of essays in English and German on a wide variety of adaptations and rewritings.

21 *The Times*, 2 July 1982.

22 A black and white BBC TV recording of the 1963 revival (which made further cuts in music and dialogue) has been reissued by DECCA (2009).

Brook. The heavily-cut script ensured that Laurence Olivier's Macheath was the centre of attention and unquestioningly the rakish hero. Peachum and Lockit were much reduced in importance, and criminals and prostitutes had little force beyond their convenience in making up a chorus for expanded 'production numbers' lushly scored by Sir Arthur Bliss.

By contrast, Jonathan Miller's 1983 BBC TV production offered a virtually complete text, with music performed in period style. Miller recorded that 'we actually rehearsed with Hogarth's drawings ... laid out in front of us',[23] and he peopled the set with silent figures engaged in historically 'authentic' activities. It offered a relatively 'straight' account of the work without quite coming to life, and if Olivier dominated the earlier film, here Roger Daltrey's Macheath had little sexual magnetism. Nonetheless the trio sung as the bell tolls for Macheath's execution had – as it almost always does in performance – a moving solemnity, and it is still for students a version much preferable to that of 1953.

A different way of dealing with the work's historical distance was attempted in David Freeman's Opera Factory realisation in 1982. This highly controversial production juxtaposed 'period' performance of much of the music with sudden switches into heavy rock and back again. Robert Henderson described it as: 'played in dilapidated everyday clothes, with a few beer crates furnishing the bare stage area, a punk, pot smoking Matt, a skinhead Macheath and a brazen Molly groping inside Macheath's underpants'.[24] If Jonathan Miller sprang a surprise by having Macheath executed at the end while his reprieve was still being discussed, Freeman went further as 'the jolly "lumps of pudding" finale became a mass hanging, a hideous twisting dance of death'.[25]

This was an extreme attempt to jolt the work – and the audience – out of a period straightjacket and complacent prettiness; others have tried in different ways to 'make repayment of Brecht's debt to Gay', to borrow a phrase from a *Times* review of Peter Wood's 1963 production, of which he wrote: 'In place of period charm or historical authenticity it puts its main emphasis on stark social comment'. The action was played out in 'a sombre prison interior. In the background rises the mast of a transportation ship, a gallows tree stands before the gate, and the prisoners lie huddled among a collection of giant packing cases scrutinized by a guard patrolling an upper gallery.' The story of Macheath then became 'a transient moment of gaiety, its happy ending swiftly followed by the return of harsh reality when they and their spectators are driven aboard

23 *Radio Times*, 29 October 1983.
24 *Daily Telegraph*, 9 January 1982.
25 Hugo Cole, *The Guardian*, 8 January 1982.

at gun point.'[26] It attracted some negative comment because it cast actors who could sing a bit rather than singers who might be able to act (Dorothy Tutin recapitulated Polly Peachum, which she played in Brook's film, but sang for herself, rather than having her singing dubbed). This has been a continuous tension since the very earliest performances.

John Caird's 1992 production in the Swan Theatre at Stratford might seem similarly dark in intention, since it began when 'hanged, hooded bodies drop startlingly from the high roof and swing aloft on ropes like some grisly ceiling decoration.'[27] But while one reviewer thought that 'instead of a period romp [Caird] offers us a picture of a vicious criminal underworld that is a mirror-image of bourgeois society',[28] another dismissively characterised it as an 'anodyne, middle-of-the-road version ... undemanding, easy theatre'.[29] The musical arrangements of Ilona Sekacz, leaning towards elaboration rather than authenticity and moving the work firmly in the direction of contemporary stage musical, contributed to the ambivalence of response. But the mixed reaction says something, too, of the way Gay's work eludes easy capture.

Richard Eyre's National Theatre production of 1982/3 was one of the most widely applauded of twentieth-century renditions.[30] Some airs were omitted (including a number of Polly's more affecting pieces), others were simplified, and new tunes occasionally substituted. The arranger, Dominic Muldowney, transposed songs in order that, as Imelda Staunton (who played Lucy Lockit) remarked, they were 'pitched for the natural ranges of the actors' voices. This means that it's much more natural when the character starts to sing.'[31] Michael Billington felt that 'instead of numbers, the songs become a continuation of drama by other means'.[32] This was a production which eschewed the operatic, or even Caird's stage-musical style. The action was relocated into the nineteenth century; Paul Jones's 'powerful performance [as Macheath] suggests an authentically dangerous man complete with a Glaswegian accent with an edge like a broken bottle'.[33] Sheridan Morley wrote that its 'real achievement has

26 *The Times*, 17 July 1963.
27 *The Independent*, 9 April 1992.
28 Michael Billington, *The Guardian*, 10 April 1992.
29 Andrew St George, *Financial Times*, 9 April 1992.
30 This production was transmitted on Channel 4 in 1983, but I have not been able to locate a copy of the recording. It would make an instructive comparison with Miller's TV production, which followed only a few months later.
31 *The Times*, 15 July 1983. Bernard Crick, in *Times Higher Education Supplement*, 16 July 1982, however, felt that this simplification removed some of the important tensions between words and music in the original.
32 Michael Billington, *The Guardian*, 7 July 1982.
33 Terry Grimley, *Birmingham Post*, 18 October 1983.

been to steer this *Beggar's Opera* away not only from the frills of the Playfair-Lyric tradition but also from the Brecht-Weill variant as well'.[34]

The Beggar's Opera continues to be frequently staged. It also continues to prompt creative responses and adaptations. This eighteenth-century runaway theatrical success, then, still stimulates and challenges writers, actors, directors – and readers – into the twenty-first century.

A Note on the Text

The textual history of *The Beggar's Opera* is a complex one. The most comprehensive description of the early editions is given in the edition by Peter Lewis (1973), and the fullest account of the music is in Jeremy Barlow's edition of 1990.

The first edition of Gay's work was issued by 14 February 1728, just over a fortnight after the first performance, in octavo format (O1). A second edition in the same format was published by 9 April 1728 (O2). Its most significant changes from the first edition were the printing of the 'overture in score', the continuous numbering of the airs and the moving of the tunes of the songs from the end of the book to immediately before the words they set. Its few substantive changes are almost certainly authorial in origin. The third edition was issued in 1729 in the larger quarto format (Q1). There is no significant modification of the text, but the music is presented quite differently, with the words for the first time printed under the notes, and a bass line added.

Since O2 includes almost certainly authorial, and manifestly superior readings, it is taken as the copy-text for the verbal element in this edition. For the music, however, the copy-text is Q1. But the music is presented here in a form which combines the melody and verbal underlay of Q1 with the location of the music above the words of the lyrics and the absence of a bass line which is characteristic of O2. To omit the music is a travesty of the originals, in which the melodies of the airs were always included, but to put the tunes alone above the words, however, as in O2, would leave the reader uncertain of how melody and lyrics go together. In a theatrical production it would be necessary to produce a full score for instrumentalists – something this edition does not aspire to do; its aim, more modestly, is to allow the interested student access to the melodies. We have chosen not to reprint the musical score of the overture, in part simply for reasons of space, but also because this, too, belongs with a full performance score, rather than this reading edition.

The spelling, punctuation and capitalisation of the original have all been modernised in line with series conventions, except that we have

34 *Punch*, 14 July 1982.

deliberately chosen to retain some few of the long dashes characteristic of eighteenth-century texts. The long dash was used in the period in a variety of ways, but especially to indicate the fluctuations of high passion. The flurry of dashes which punctuates Polly's fevered imaginings of Macheath's execution in I.xii, for example, typographically underscores the heightened emotions she expresses. At other points a dash enables a sudden turn of thought, or acts as a suggestion to the actor to pause. Where these indications seem particularly useful to the modern reader dashes have been retained, though many more have silently been modified.

FURTHER READING

Bindman, David and Scott Wilcox, eds., *"Among the Whores and Thieves": William Hogarth and The Beggar's Opera*, 1997.

Bloom, Harold, ed., *John Gay's The Beggar's Opera: Modern Critical Interpretations*, 1988.

Booth, Mark W., *The Experience of Songs*, 1981, pp. 115–24.

Brecht, Bertolt, *The Threepenny Opera*, translated by Ralph Mannheim and John Willett, 1979.

Denning, Michael, 'Beggars and Thieves: the Ideology of the Gang', *Literature and History*, 8 (1982), pp. 41–55; reprinted in Bloom, pp. 99–116.

Donaldson, Ian, *The World Upside-Down: Comedy from Jonson to Fielding*, 1970, pp. 159–82; reprinted in Noble, pp. 65–79.

Donohue, Joseph, ed., *The Cambridge History of British Theatre Vol. 2, 1660 to 1895*, 2004, 'Introduction: the theatre from 1660 to 1800', pp. 3–52.

Dugaw, Dianne, *"Deep Play": John Gay and the Invention of Modernity*, 2001.

————, 'The Politics of Culture: John Gay and Popular Ballads', in Tom Cheesman and Sigrid Rieuwerts, eds., *Ballads into Books: The Legacies of Francis James Child*, 1999, pp. 189–98.

Empson, William, *Some Versions of Pastoral*, 1935, pp. 195–250, reprinted in Bloom, pp. 5–36, and, abbreviated, in Noble, pp. 15–40.

Fiske, Roger, *English Theatre Music in the Eighteenth Century*, 2nd ed., 1986.

Guinerot, J. V. and Rodney D. Jilg, eds., *Contexts 1: The Beggar's Opera*, 1976.

McIntosh, William A., 'Handel, Walpole and Gay: The Aims of *The Beggar's Opera*', *Eighteenth–Century Studies*, 7 (1974), pp. 415–33; reprinted in Bloom, pp. 65–80.

McNeff, Stephen '*The Threepenny Opera*', in Peter Thomson and Glendyr Sacks, eds., *The Cambridge Companion to Brecht*, 2nd ed., 2006, pp. 78–89.

Newman, Steve, *Ballad Collection, Lyric, and the Canon*, 2007, pp. 15–43.

Nicholson, Colin, *Writing and the Rise of Finance: Capital Satires of the Early Eighteenth Century*, 1994, pp. 123–38.

Noble, Yvonne, ed., *Twentieth Century Interpretations of The Beggar's Opera*, 1975.

Nokes, David, *John Gay: A Profession of Friendship*, 1995.

O'Shaughnessy, Toni-Lynn, 'A Single Capacity in *The Beggar's Opera*', *Eighteenth-Century Studies*, 21 (1987–88), pp. 212–27.

Piper, William Bowman, 'Similitude as Satire in *The Beggar's Opera*', *Eighteenth-Century Studies*, 21 (1988), pp. 334–351.

Schultz, William E., *Gay's Beggar's Opera : its Content, History and Influence*, 1923.

Winton, Calhoun, *John Gay and the London Theatre*, 1993.

————, '*The Beggar's Opera*: A case study' in Donohue, pp. 126–44.

ABBREVIATIONS

Editions of *The Beggar's Opera* cited in the Introduction and commentary are those of Peter Elfed Lewis, 1973; Brian Loughrey and T. O. Treadwell, 1986; Edgar V. Roberts, 1968; the edition of the music referred to is by Jeremy Barlow, 1990.

O1	*The beggar's opera. As it is acted at the Theatre-Royal in Lincolns-Inn-Fields. Written by Mr. Gay. To which is added, the musick engrav'd on copper-plates.* (London, 1728)
O2	*The beggar's opera. As it is acted at the Theatre-Royal in Lincolns-Inn-Fields. Written by Mr. Gay. The second edition, with the musick prefix'd to each song.* (London, 1728)
Q1	*The beggar's opera. As it is acted at the Theatre-Royal in Lincolns-Inn Fields. Written by Mr. Gay. The third edition: with the ouverture in score, the songs, and the basses, (the ouverture and basses compos'd by Dr. Pepusch) curiously engrav'd on copper plates.* (London, 1729).
Barlow	*The Music of The Beggar's Opera*, ed. Jeremy Barlow (Oxford: Oxford University Press 1990)
Lewis	*The Beggar's Opera*, ed. Peter Elfed Lewis (Edinburgh: Oliver and Boyd, 1973)
OED	*Oxford English Dictionary Online*. Oxford University Press. <http://dictionary.oed.com>

Title-page from the copy in the Brotherton Library,
University of Leeds

THE
BEGGAR's
OPERA.

As it is Acted at the

THEATRE-ROYAL

IN

LINCOLNS-INN-FIELDS.

Written by Mr. *G A Y.*

——*Nos hæc novimus esse nihil.*   Mart.

The SECOND EDITION:

To which is Added

The OUVERTURE in SCORE;
And the MUSICK *prefix'd to each* SONG.

LONDON:

Printed for JOHN WATTS, at the Printing-Office
in *Wild-Court*, near *Lincoln's-Inn-Fields.*

MDCCXXVIII.
[Price 1s. 6d.]

DRAMATIS PERSONAE

MEN

MR PEACHUM		*Mr Hippesley*	
LOCKIT		*Mr Hall*	
MACHEATH		*Mr Walker*	
FILCH		*Mr Clark*	
JEMMY TWITCHER		*Mr H Bullock*	5
CROOK-FINGERED JACK		*Mr Houghton*	
WAT DREARY		*Mr Smith*	
ROBIN OF BAGSHOT	Macheath's Gang	*Mr Lacy*	
NIMMING NED		*Mr Pit*	
HARRY PADINGTON		*Mr Eaton*	10
MATT OF THE MINT		*Mr Spiller*	
BEN BUDGE		*Mr Morgan*	
BEGGAR		*Mr Chapman*	
PLAYER		*Mr Milward*	

CONSTABLES, TURNKEYS, DRAWER, [MEMBERS OF   15
MACHEATH'S GANG, HARPER, SERVANT, PRISONERS, JAILOR]

WOMEN

MRS PEACHUM		*Mrs Martin*	
POLLY PEACHUM		*Miss Fenton*	
LUCY LOCKIT		*Mrs Egleton*	
DIANA TRAPES		*Mrs Martin*	20
MRS COAXER		*Mrs Holiday*	
DOLLY TRULL		*Mrs Lacy*	
MRS VIXEN		*Mrs Rice*	
BETTY DOXY	Women of the Town	*Mrs Rogers*	
JENNY DIVER		*Mrs Clarke*	25
MRS SLAMMEKIN		*Mrs Morgan*	
SUKEY TAWDREY		*Mrs Palin*	
MOLLY BRAZEN		*Mrs Sallee*	

[FOUR WOMEN AND CHILDREN]

From the Second Edition onwards 'A Table of the Airs' listing the titles of all the songs, was
printed at the front of the text.

0   *DRAMATIS PERSONAE* The names of the actors in the first performances continued to be printed for some time after the cast changed. In some copies of the Second Edition an additional cast of 'Lilliputians' (a children's company which gave sixteen performances in 1729) was also included. This is not reproduced here.

1   *PEACHUM* Means 'Peach 'em'. To 'peach' is 1) to accuse formally 2) to give evidence against, to betray.

2   *LOCKIT* an appropriate name for the chief jailer at Newgate prison.

3   *MACHEATH* a Scottish name-form, meaning 'son of the heath'. Highwaymen commonly sought their victims travelling on the heaths around London.
    Mr Walker the actor and comedian, Thomas Walker (1698–1744), well-known in the London theatre and at summer fairs. Though not originally intended for him, the role of Macheath made his career. Walker appears in William Hogarth's illustration of the prison scene (III.xi) and a popular print of the time showing Walker as Macheath decorates the harlot's squalid room in Plate 3 of Hogarth's *A Harlot's Progress* (1732) (see Introduction, p. xix).

4   *FILCH* to steal; also the name of a long hooked implement used to thieve from open windows.

5   *TWITCHER* a pickpocket.

8   *ROBIN OF BAGSHOT* Bagshot Heath was notorious for highwaymen, but the name is also a satirical allusion to the first minister and Chancellor of the Exchequer Robert Walpole (see commentary on I.iii.27–8 and Introduction, p. xv–xvi).

9   *NIMMING* To 'nim' is 'to steal, or whip off or away any thing' (*New Canting Dictionary*, 1725).

10   *HARRY PADINGTON* also called 'Henry' in II.i. A 'pad' is 'the highway; also a robber thereon' (*New Canting Dictionary*, 1725): in other words, a highwayman. Paddington, then on the outskirts of London, was the parish in which stood the gallows at Tyburn.

11   *MATT OF THE MINT* The 'Mint' was a district in Southwark notorious as a haven for criminals.

12   *BUDGE* a thief: 'One that slips into an House in the dark, and taking Cloaks, Coats, or what comes next to Hand, marches off with them' (*New Canting Dictionary*, 1725).

15   *DRAWER* 'One who draws liquor for customers; a tapster at a tavern' (*OED*).
    Miss Fenton Lavinia Fenton (1710–1760), actress and singer, and later Duchess of Bolton, is said to have been largely responsible for the success of the first production, delighting audiences with her representation of Polly as innocent and virtuous. She attained great celebrity. A mezzotint portrait of Fenton as Polly was hugely popular, her 'lives' were published, and her image appeared on screens and fans. Before the end of the first production run she eloped with the Earl of Bolton whom Hogarth depicts staring admiringly at her in his painting illustrating Act III, scene xi (see also Introduction, p. xix).

20   *TRAPES* 'A dangling slattern' (*New Canting Dictionary*, 1725); a slovenly woman.

22   *TRULL* a prostitute.

24   *DOXY* mistress of a criminal, hence a prostitute. According to the *New Canting Dictionary*, doxies are 'She-beggars, Trulls, Wenches, Whores . . . being neither Maids, Wives, nor Widows, [they] will, for good Victuals, or a small Piece of Money, prostitute their Bodies, protesting they never did so before'.

25   *DIVER* a pickpocket.

26   *SLAMMEKIN* an untidy, slovenly woman.

27   *TAWDREY* implies 'dressed in cheap finery'. 'Tawdry lace' was originally the name of a silk necktie, named after St Audrey, and sold at her fair.

INTRODUCTION

[*Enter*] BEGGAR [*and*] PLAYER

BEGGAR

If poverty be a title to poetry, I am sure nobody can dispute
mine. I own myself of the Company of Beggars; and I make one
at their weekly festivals at St Giles's. I have a small yearly salary
for my catches, and am welcome to a dinner there whenever I
please, which is more than most poets can say.   5

PLAYER

As we live by the Muses, 'tis but a gratitude in us to encourage
poetical merit wherever we find it. The Muses, contrary to all
other ladies, pay no distinction to dress, and never partially
mistake the pertness of embroidery for wit, nor the modesty of
want for dullness. Be the author who he will, we push his play as   10
far as it will go. So, though you are in want, I wish you success
heartily.

BEGGAR

This piece, I own, was originally writ for the celebrating the
marriage of James Chanter and Moll Lay, two most excellent
ballad-singers. I have introduced the similes that are in all your   15

1   *title* 'confers a right to' (*OED* title, *n*.6).
2   *the Company of Beggars* suggesting that beggars are organised and have the status
    of the ancient trade guilds or 'City Companies'.
3   *weekly festivals at St Giles's* The parish of St Giles in the Fields, off the modern
    Charing Cross Road, was an area where many recent migrants to London lived.
    Also known as 'the Rookery', it became synonymous with crime and 'St Giles's
    Greek' was thieves' cant associated with the area. The 'weekly festivals' might refer
    to the procession of condemned prisoners to the gallows at Tyburn (see
    commentary on I.xii.1–6) which happened on most Mondays of the year and
    which stopped at the Angel Inn where prisoners were offered a last drink.
4   *catches* songs in the form of a round, where each voice enters with the same tune
    in turn. Catches were intended to be sung in all-male gatherings, and the words,
    therefore, are often to do with drinking or sex.
6   *the Muses* classical goddesses, patrons of the arts and sciences.
8   *partially* unfairly.
9   *pertness of embroidery* The player compares elaborately (and the implication is,
    extravagantly) decorated garments with over-ingenious poetry.
10 *want* poverty.
14–15 *James . . . ballad-singers* generic fictional names. Ballads on many subjects were sold
    cheaply, and peddled by singers who had a reputation for gathering crowds to pick
    their pockets, as Gay points out in *Trivia*: 'Guard well thy pocket; for these *Syrens*

celebrated operas: the swallow, the moth, the bee, the ship, the flower, etcetera. Besides, I have a prison-scene, which the ladies always reckon charmingly pathetic. As to the parts, I have observed such a nice impartiality to our two ladies that it is impossible for either of them to take offence. I hope I may be forgiven, that I have not made my opera throughout unnatural, like those in vogue; for I have no recitative. Excepting this, as I have consented to have neither prologue nor epilogue, it must be allowed an opera in all its forms. The piece indeed hath been heretofore frequently represented by ourselves in our great room at St Giles's, so that I cannot too often acknowledge your charity in bringing it now on the stage.

PLAYER

But now I see 'tis time for us to withdraw; the actors are preparing to begin. Play away the overture!

[*Exeunt*]

[*The Overture*]

stand / To aid the labours of the diving hand' (III. 79–80). Like Gay's lyrics, ballads were usually written to fit existing tunes.

17   *a prison-scene* Set largely in Newgate, Gay's burlesque has rather more than the single prison-scene which was virtually obligatory in contemporary Italian operas.

18–20   *As . . . offence* Alluding to the celebrated quarrels between the two operatic leading ladies of the period, Faustina Bordoni and Francesca Cuzzoni, and possibly to Handel's unsuccessful attempt to reconcile them by providing them with equally strong roles in his opera *Alessandro* (1726).

22   *recitative* prose dialogue between arias set to music half-way between melody and speech. English audiences were initially bewildered by this Italian operatic convention.

23   *prologue . . . epilogue* It was usual for eighteenth-century plays to have a prologue and an epilogue, but not for operas to do so.

25–6   *great room at St Giles's* It is tempting to identify this with the St Giles's Roundhouse, a temporary prison for suspected criminals, from which Jack Sheppard (see Introduction, p. xv) escaped in 1724.

29   *overture* the substantial instrumental prelude composed by Johann Christoph Pepusch, musical director of the Theatre Royal; it was printed in the second and subsequent editions, scored for strings, oboes, and continuo, but is not reproduced here, principally for reasons of space.

ACT I, SCENE i

Scene, PEACHUM's *house*

PEACHUM *sitting at a table with a large book of accounts before him*

Air 1   An Old Woman Clothed in Gray   [Anon]

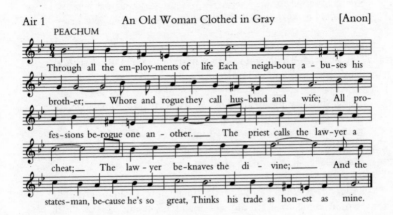

PEACHUM

Through all the employments of life Each neighbour abuses his brother; Whore and rogue they call husband and wife; All professions be-rogue one another. The priest calls the lawyer a cheat; The lawyer be-knaves the divine; And the statesman, because he's so great, Thinks his trade as honest as mine.

PEACHUM

Through all the employments of life
    Each neighbour abuses his brother;
Whore and rogue they call husband and wife;
    All professions be-rogue one another.
The priest calls the lawyer a cheat;   5
    The lawyer be-knaves the divine;
And the statesman, because he's so great,
    Thinks his trade as honest as mine.

PEACHUM

A lawyer is an honest employment; so is mine. Like me too he
acts in a double capacity, both against rogues and for 'em; for 'tis   10

---

0 s.d. 1 *Scene* Each scene would have been played against a painted backdrop (see
    Introduction, p. xxiii).
    Air 1 An . . . Gray The title refers to the first line of a ballad narrating the seduction
    of a trusting girl. The tune itself was also known as 'Unconstant Roger'. Both
    probably date from the seventeenth century.
4, 6 *be-rogue, be-knave* call one another 'rogues'; calls him 'knave'.

7

but fitting that we should protect and encourage cheats, since we live by them.

[ACT I,] SCENE ii

PEACHUM [*remains; to him enter*] FILCH

FILCH

Sir, Black Moll hath sent word her trial comes on in the afternoon, and she hopes you will order matters so as to bring her off.

PEACHUM

Why, she may plead her belly at worst; to my knowledge she hath taken care of that security. But as the wench is very active and industrious, you may satisfy her that I'll soften the evidence. 5

FILCH

Tom Gagg, sir, is found guilty.

PEACHUM

A lazy dog! When I took him the time before, I told him what he would come to if he did not mend his hand. This is death without reprieve. I may venture to book him. (*Writes*) 'For Tom Gagg, forty pounds'. Let Betty Sly know that I'll save her from 10 transportation, for I can get more by her staying in England.

FILCH

Betty hath brought more goods into our lock to-year than any

---

2 *bring her off* ensure she is found not guilty.
3 *plead her belly* claim pregnancy. Convicted women could not be executed while pregnant. They were often transported instead, though some were hanged once the baby was delivered. The implication here is that Black Moll has deliberately got pregnant to avoid execution. *M. Misson's Memoirs* (1719), pp. 329–30, report that 'very often they declare that they are with child, and often too the poor criminals are so indeed; for tho' they came never so good virgins into the prison, there are a set of wags there that take care of those matters' (see also III.iii.4–6 and note).
8 *took* apprehended and brought to justice.
9 *mend his hand* improve his work or conduct (*OED* hand 4).
10 *forty pounds* the reward for information leading to conviction; it was offered for reporting male, but not female criminals (see 18–20 below).
11 *transportation* Transportation to the colonies in America and the West Indies could be for life or for fixed periods of years, usually seven or fourteen. See II.i.2.
12 *lock* warehouse for stolen goods (see Gay's note to III.iii.13).
    to-year year by year.

five of the gang; and in truth, 'tis a pity to lose so good a customer.

PEACHUM

If none of the gang take her off, she may, in the common course   15
of business, live a twelvemonth longer. I love to let women
'scape. A good sportsman always lets the hen partridges fly,
because the breed of the game depends upon them. Besides,
here the law allows us no reward; there is nothing to be got by
the death of women – except our wives.   20

FILCH

Without dispute, she is a fine woman! 'Twas to her I was obliged
for my education, and (to say a bold word) she hath trained up
more young fellows to the business than the gaming table.

PEACHUM

Truly, Filch, thy observation is right. We and the surgeons are
more beholden to women than all the professions besides.   25

Air 2   The Bonny Gray-Eyed Morn   [Jeremiah Clarke]

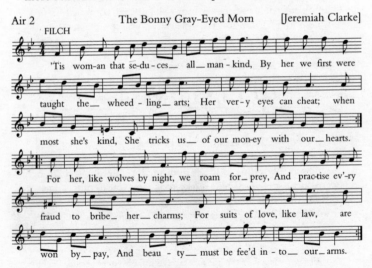

'Tis wom-an that se-du-ces all man-kind, By her we first were taught the wheed-ling arts; Her ver-y eyes can cheat; when most she's kind, She tricks us of our mon-ey with our hearts. For her, like wolves by night, we roam for prey, And prac-tise ev'-ry fraud to bribe her charms; For suits of love, like law, are won by pay, And beau-ty must be fee'd in-to our arms.

15   *take her off* get her executed (by informing against her).
22–3   *education . . . table* 'the business' to which both Betty and gambling lead young men
    is crime, though Betty might also provide sexual initiation.
24–5   *surgeons . . . women* 'Surgeon' in the early eighteenth century could be used simply
    to describe a general medical practitioner, often with limited qualifications. Quack
    medical practitioners who claimed expertise in treating venereal disease, which
    men are here assumed to catch from prostitutes, were particularly prevalent.

FILCH

'Tis woman that seduces all mankind,
  By her we first were taught the wheedling arts;
Her very eyes can cheat; when most she's kind,
  She tricks us of our money with our hearts.
For her, like wolves by night, we roam for prey,   30
  And practise ev'ry fraud to bribe her charms;
For suits of love, like law, are won by pay,
  And beauty must be fee'd into our arms.

PEACHUM

But make haste to Newgate, boy, and let my friends know what
I intend, for I love to make them easy one way or other.   35

FILCH

When a gentleman is long kept in suspense, penitence may
break his spirit ever after. Besides, certainty gives a man a good
air upon his trial, and makes him risk another without fear or
scruple. But I'll away, for 'tis a pleasure to be the messenger of
comfort to friends in affliction.   [*Exit*]   40

[ACT I,] SCENE iii

PEACHUM [*remains, alone*]

PEACHUM

But 'tis now high time to look about me for a decent execution
against next sessions. I hate a lazy rogue, by whom one can get
nothing till he is hanged. (*Reading*) 'A register of the gang.
Crook-fingered Jack': a year and a half in the service. Let me

---

25 *Air 2 The Bonny . . . Morn* The tune takes its name from the opening line of 'A New
  Scotch Song' which may have been theatrical in origin. It was used in a number of
  ballad operas after Gay's, and attached to many other broadsides. Its narrative is a
  conventional one of male seduction, which Filch reverses by laying blame on women.
33 *beauty . . . arms* We must pay women to accept our embraces.
34 *Newgate* London's principal prison, situated close to the criminal court of the Old
  Bailey.
38 *air* appearance, manner.

2 *sessions* the criminal trials held eight times a year at the Old Bailey.

see how much the stock owes to his industry: one, two, three, four, five gold watches, and seven silver ones. A mighty clean-handed fellow! Sixteen snuff-boxes, five of them of true gold. Six dozen of handkerchiefs, four silver-hilted swords, half a dozen of shirts, three tie-periwigs and a piece of broadcloth. Considering these are only the fruits of his leisure hours, I don't know a prettier fellow, for no man alive hath a more engaging presence of mind upon the road. 'Wat Dreary, alias Brown Will': an irregular dog, who hath an underhand way of disposing of his goods. I'll try him only for a sessions or two longer upon his good behaviour. 'Harry Padington': a poor petty-larceny rascal, without the least genius; that fellow, though he were to live these six months, will never come to the gallows with any credit. 'Slippery Sam': he goes off the next sessions, for the villain hath the impudence to have views of following his trade as a tailor, which he calls an honest employment. 'Matt of the Mint': listed not above a month ago, a promising sturdy fellow, and diligent in his way; somewhat too bold and hasty, and may raise good contributions on the public, if he does not cut himself short by murder. 'Tom Tipple': a guzzling, soaking sot, who is always too drunk to stand himself, or to make others stand. A cart is absolutely necessary for him. 'Robin of Bagshot, alias Gorgon, alias Bob Bluff, alias Carbuncle, alias Bob Booty'.

5

10

15

20

25

---

7   *snuff-boxes* containers for powdered tobacco. The vogue for taking snuff began in the late seventeenth century. Snuff-boxes were often expensive and fashionable items.

8–9   *handkerchiefs . . . broadcloth* items prized by thieves and indicative of fashion as a sign of wealth and status. Handkerchiefs, worn by women round the neck, were made of valuable fabrics and often highly decorated; tie-periwigs, worn by men, had hair gathered back and held with a black ribbon; broadcloth was a fine quality cloth used for men's clothes.

10   *leisure hours* implying that he had a 'legitimate' job during the day.

13–14   *underhand . . . goods* i.e. to someone other than Peachum.

16   *petty-larceny* theft of goods worth less than 1 shilling (5 pence in modern coinage). A non-capital offence.

26   *cart* used to transport prisoners to the gallows.

27–8   *Robin of Bagshot . . . Bob Booty* aliases taken by contemporaries to be satirical references to the first minister, Sir Robert Walpole. The suggestions are that he is a monster, an excrescence ('carbuncle') on the body politic and a robber of the nation. 'Bob' is a slang term for a 'Shop-lift's Comerade [sic], Assistant, or Receiver' (*New Canting Dictionary*, 1725) (see also Introduction, p. xv).

[ACT I,] SCENE iv

PEACHUM [*remains; to him enter*] MRS PEACHUM

MRS PEACHUM

What of Bob Booty, husband? I hope nothing bad hath betided him. You know, my dear, he's a favourite customer of mine. 'Twas he made me a present of this ring.

PEACHUM

I have set his name down in the black list, that's all, my dear; he spends his life among women, and as soon as his money is gone, 5 one or other of the ladies will hang him for the reward, and there's forty pounds lost to us forever.

MRS PEACHUM

You know, my dear, I never meddle in matters of death; I always leave those affairs to you. Women indeed are bitter bad judges in these cases, for they are so partial to the brave that they 10 think every man handsome who is going to the camp or the gallows.

Air 3   Cold and Raw   [Anon]

If a-ny wench Venus's gir-dle wear, Though she be nev-er so
ug-ly, Lil-ies and ros-es will quick-ly ap-pear, And her face look
won-drous smug-ly. smug-ly. Be-neath the left ear so fit but a
cord (A rope so charm-ing a zone is!), The youth in his cart hath the
air of a lord, And we cry:— 'There dies an A-don-is!'

4   *black list* the record of those he intends to send to the gallows.
5   *spends . . . women* Walpole notoriously had a mistress, Maria Skerrett.
9   *bitter bad* extremely poor.
12   *Air 3 Cold and Raw* a new title given to an old tune, originally known as 'Stingo', or 'Oil of Barley', after it became associated with this first line of a ballad by D'Urfey. Widely used in ballads and in the theatre.

MRS PEACHUM
If any wench Venus's girdle wear,
   Though she be never so ugly,
Lilies and roses will quickly appear,   15
   And her face look wondrous smugly.
Beneath the left ear so fit but a cord
   (A rope so charming a zone is!)
The youth in his cart hath the air of a lord,
   And we cry: 'There dies an Adonis!'   20

MRS PEACHUM

But really, husband, you should not be too hard-hearted, for you never had a finer, braver set of men than at present. We have not had a murder among them all these seven months. And truly, my dear, that is a great blessing.

PEACHUM

What a dickens is the woman always a-whimpering about   25 murder for? No gentleman is ever looked upon the worse for killing a man in his own defence; and if business cannot be carried on without it, what would you have a gentleman do?

MRS PEACHUM

If I am in the wrong, my dear, you must excuse me, for nobody can help the frailty of an over-scrupulous conscience.   30

PEACHUM

Murder is as fashionable a crime as a man can be guilty of. How many fine gentlemen have we in Newgate every year, purely upon that article! If they have wherewithal to persuade the jury to bring it in manslaughter, what are they the worse for it? So, my dear, have done upon this subject. Was Captain   35 Macheath here this morning for the banknotes he left with you last week?

MRS PEACHUM

Yes, my dear; and though the bank hath stopped payment, he

13–20   *Venus's girdle . . . cord . . . Adonis* In Roman mythology Venus, goddess of love, had a girdle, or 'zone', which made its wearer instantly desirable just as, the song suggests, the hangman's noose makes a man into an Adonis, the beautiful youth tragically beloved of Venus.

16   *smugly* handsomely, without the more modern sense of conceitedly.

25   *a dickens* the devil.

36   *banknotes* at this period, receipts for money deposited in a bank but payable to the bearer, so used as currency. A thief could cash such a note provided he moved quickly, before a stop-payment notice was sent to the bank.

was so cheerful and so agreeable! Sure there is not a finer gentleman upon the road than the Captain! If he comes from 40 Bagshot at any reasonable hour he hath promised to make one this evening with Polly and me and Bob Booty at a party of quadrille. Pray, my dear, is the Captain rich?

PEACHUM

The Captain keeps too good company ever to grow rich. Marybone and the chocolate-houses are his undoing. The man 45 that proposes to get money by play should have the education of a fine gentleman, and be trained up to it from his youth.

MRS PEACHUM

Really, I am sorry upon Polly's account the Captain hath not more discretion. What business hath he to keep company with lords and gentlemen? He should leave them to prey upon one 50 another.

PEACHUM

Upon Polly's account! What a plague does the woman mean? Upon Polly's account!

MRS PEACHUM

Captain Macheath is very fond of the girl.

PEACHUM

And what then? 55

MRS PEACHUM

If I have any skill in the ways of women, I am sure Polly thinks him a very pretty man.

PEACHUM

And what then? You would not be so mad as to have the wench marry him! Gamesters and highwaymen are generally very good to their whores, but they are very devils to their wives. 60

MRS PEACHUM

But if Polly should be in love, how should we help her, or how can she help herself? Poor girl, I am in the utmost concern about her.

---

41 *Bagshot* See commentary on *Dramatis Personae.*
43 *quadrille* a four-handed card game popular in the 1720s.
45 *Marybone . . . houses* Marylebone pleasure gardens were one of London's main gambling centres and gambling was also a popular pastime at the fashionable chocolate houses where men met to gossip over cocoa. The form 'Marybone' is not merely a spelling variant; it reflects the original form of the name of the district. The '-*le*-' was only added in the later 17th century.

14

Air 4   Why is your Faithful Slave Disdained?   [Buononcini]

If love the virgin's heart invade. How like a moth the simple maid Still plays about the flame! flame! If soon she be not made a wife, Her honour's singed, and then for life She's—what I dare not name.

MRS PEACHUM

If love the virgin's heart invade,
How like a moth the simple maid   65
   Still plays about the flame!
If soon she be not made a wife,
Her honour's singed, and then for life
   She's – what I dare not name.

PEACHUM

Look ye, wife. A handsome wench in our way of business is as   70
profitable as at the bar of a Temple coffee-house, who looks
upon it as her livelihood to grant every liberty but one. You see
I would indulge the girl as far as prudently we can. In anything
but marriage! After that, my dear, how shall we be safe? Are we
not then in her husband's power? For a husband hath the   75
absolute power over all a wife's secrets but her own. If the girl
had the discretion of a court-lady, who can have a dozen young
fellows at her ear without complying with one, I should not
matter it; but Polly is tinder, and a spark will at once set her on
a flame. Married! If the wench does not know her own profit,   80

63   *Air 4 Why . . . Disdained* The title is the first line of a song first appearing in 1688
     with a different tune. It is a lyric of male desire in which the speaker pleads for the
     possession 'Of what I dare not name' – the line towards which Gay's lyric heads.
     This tune has been attributed to Buononcini, though no specific source is identified.
71   *a Temple coffee-house* Like the chocolate houses, coffee-houses were sites of male
     sociability where women were mainly restricted to serving behind the counter.
     Particular coffee-houses were associated with specific professions or political
     allegiances. The Temple coffee-house took its name from the Middle and Inner
     Temple Inns of Court near which it was situated.
79   *matter it* be concerned about it.

sure she knows her own pleasure better than to make herself a
property! My daughter to me should be, like a court-lady to a
minister of state, a key to the whole gang. Married! If the affair
is not already done, I'll terrify her from it, by the example of our
neighbours.   85

MRS PEACHUM

Mayhap, my dear, you may injure the girl. She loves to imitate
the fine ladies, and she may only allow the Captain liberties in
the view of interest.

PEACHUM

But 'tis your duty, my dear, to warn the girl against her ruin, and
to instruct her how to make the most of her beauty. I'll go to her   90
this moment, and sift her. In the meantime, wife, rip out the
coronets and marks of these dozen of cambric handkerchiefs,
for I can dispose of them this afternoon to a chap in the City.

[*Exit*]

[ACT I,] SCENE v

MRS PEACHUM [*remains, alone*]

MRS PEACHUM

Never was a man more out of the way in an argument than my
husband! Why must our Polly, forsooth, differ from her sex, and
love only her husband? And why must Polly's marriage,
contrary to all observation, make her the less followed by other
men? All men are thieves in love, and like a woman the better for   5
being another's property.

81–2   *make herself a property* Under the law of 'coverture', which stood in English law
       until the Married Women's Property Acts of 1870 and 1882, a married woman's
       possessions, earnings and, in effect, her body were the property of her husband.
82–3   *like a court-lady . . . state* alluding to the political influence of women at the royal
       court in general and, more particularly, to Walpole as a favourite of Queen Caroline.
87–8   *in . . . interest* in order to gain something.
91   *sift* interrogate closely.
92   *coronets . . . cambric* embroidered decorations identifying the owner. Cambric is
       fine white linen.
93   *chap* customer, dealer (abbreviation of 'chapman').

4   *observation* 'rule gathered by experience' (*OED* 6)

Air 5   Of All the Simple Things We Do   [Anon]

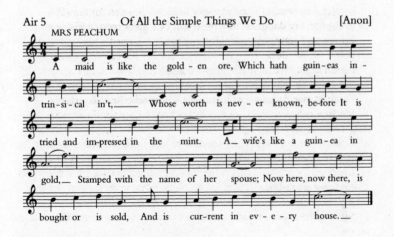

MRS PEACHUM

A maid is like the golden ore,
Which hath guineas intrinsical in't,
    Whose worth is never known, before
It is tried and impressed in the mint.   10
    A wife's like a guinea in gold,
Stamped with the name of her spouse;
    Now here, now there, is bought or is sold,
And is current in every house.

[ACT I,] SCENE vi

MRS PEACHUM [*remains; to her enter*] FILCH

MRS PEACHUM

Come hither, Filch. [*Aside*] I am as fond of this child, as though
my mind misgave me he were my own. He hath as fine a hand
at picking a pocket as a woman, and is as nimble-fingered as a

6   *Air 5 Of . . . Do* The first line of a ballad, probably by D'Urfey, which may have
    originated in Thomas Doggett's play, *The Country-Wake* (1696). It is a lyric of
    complaint against the fetters of marriage, an ironic counterpoint to the lyric here.
10 *tried and impressed* refined and stamped (the image is of making coinage).

juggler. [*To* FILCH] If an unlucky session does not cut the rope
of thy life, I pronounce, boy, thou wilt be a great man in history. 5
Where was your post last night, my boy?

FILCH

I plied at the Opera, madam; and considering 'twas neither dark
nor rainy, so that there was no great hurry in getting chairs and
coaches, made a tolerable hand on't. These seven handkerchiefs,
Madam. 10

MRS PEACHUM

Coloured ones, I see. They are of sure sale from our warehouse
at Redriff among the seamen.

FILCH

And this snuff-box.

MRS PEACHUM

Set in gold! A pretty encouragement this to a young beginner.

FILCH

I had a fair tug at charming gold watch. Pox take the tailors for 15
making the fobs so deep and narrow! It stuck by the way, and I
was forced to make my escape under a coach. Really, Madam, I
fear I shall be cut off in the flower of my youth, so that every
now and then (since I was pumped) I have thoughts of taking
up and going to sea. 20

MRS PEACHUM

You should go to Hockley in the Hole, and to Marybone, child,
to learn valour. These are the schools that have bred so many

---

4   *juggler* conjuror, demonstrating sleight of hand (rather than later sense of
    throwing and catching objects).
7   *plied* practised my trade.
    Opera The King's Theatre, in the Haymarket, known as The Opera House.
8   *chairs* sedan chairs, closed vehicles for one person, carried on poles by two bearers,
    which were available for public hire.
12 *Redriff* Rotherhithe, south of the Thames, an area of docks and shipyards. This
    17th-century variant form of the name is still preserved in a street name in the
    district.
16 *fobs* small pockets in breeches for holding watches or other valuables.
19 *pumped* put under the cold water pump: rough justice administered to pickpockets
    caught red-handed. Compare Gay's *Trivia* (1716) 'Seiz'd by rough hands, he's
    dragged amid the rout, / And stretch'd beneath the pump's incessant spout'
    (III.73–4).
19–20 *taking up* enlisting.
21 *Hockley in the Hole* in Clerkenwell, site of a famous bear-garden and centre for
    other violent sports associated with the lower classes, including cock and dog-
    fighting, bull-baiting and forms of self-defence.

brave men. I thought, boy, by this time thou hadst lost fear as
well as shame. Poor lad! How little does he know yet of the Old
Bailey! For the first fact I'll insure thee from being hanged; and   25
going to sea, Filch, will come time enough upon a sentence of
transportation. But now, since you have nothing better to do,
ev'n go to your book, and learn your catechism; for really a man
makes but an ill figure in the Ordinary's paper, who cannot give
a satisfactory answer to his questions. But hark you, my lad: 30
don't tell me a lie, for you know that I hate a liar. Do you know
of anything that hath passed between Captain Macheath and
our Polly?

FILCH

I beg you, madam, don't ask me; for I must either tell a lie to you
or to Miss Polly; for I promised her I would not tell.   35

MRS PEACHUM

But when the honour of our family is concerned –

FILCH

I shall lead a sad life with Miss Polly if ever she comes to know
that I told you. Besides, I would not willingly forfeit my own
honour by betraying anybody.

MRS PEACHUM

Yonder comes my husband and Polly. Come, Filch, you shall go   40
with me into my own room, and tell me the whole story. I'll give
thee a glass of a most delicious cordial that I keep for my own
drinking.

[*Exeunt*]

24–5   *Old Bailey* London's criminal court.
  25   *fact* deed, criminal act (*OED* 1c).
28–9   *go to your book . . . catechism . . . Ordinary's paper* The Ordinary was the Chaplain
        of Newgate whose job it was to prepare condemned prisoners for death and to test
        criminals pleading 'benefit of clergy', a reduced sentence available to first offenders
        who could prove they were literate by reading a passage, usually the beginning of
        Psalm 51, from the Bible ('book'). The catechism is a set of questions and answers
        on the fundamentals of the Christian faith, but is used here to refer more generally
        to the Ordinary's interrogation. The 'Ordinary's paper', which published the
        supposed confessions of condemned criminals, was a popular sensational
        publication.
  42   *glass . . . cordial* O2; 'most delicious Glass of a Cordial' O1.

[ACT I,] SCENE vii

[Enter] PEACHUM *[and]* POLLY

POLLY

I know as well as any of the fine ladies how to make the most of myself and of my man too. A woman knows how to be mercenary, though she hath never been in a court or at an assembly. We have it in our natures, papa. If I allow Captain Macheath some trifling liberties, I have this watch and other visible marks of his favour to show for it. A girl who cannot grant some things, and refuse what is most material, will make but a poor hand of her beauty, and soon be thrown upon the common.

5

Air 6   What shall I Do to Show how Much I Love Her [Henry Purcell]

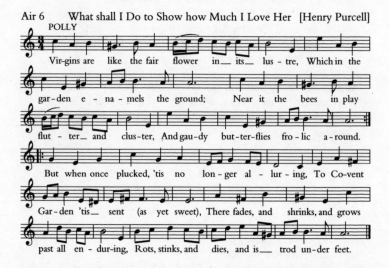

Vir-gins are like the fair flower in its lus-tre, Which in the
gar-den e - na - mels the ground; Near it the bees in play
flut - ter and clus-ter, And gau-dy but-ter-flies fro - lic a - round.
But when once plucked, 'tis no lon - ger al - lur - ing, To Co-vent
Gar-den 'tis sent (as yet sweet), There fades, and shrinks, and grows
past all en - dur-ing, Rots, stinks, and dies, and is trod un-der feet.

3–4   *court . . . assembly* gatherings for the rich and fashionable. Social events for the elite were held at the royal court. Public assemblies, which attracted a wider social mix, provided opportunities for dancing, card-playing, match-making and general sociability, and were governed by strict rules of behaviour.

8–9   *upon the common* The phrase supports Polly's claim to be able to match the self-interest of the social elite. The alternative would be to become common property, i.e. to fall into prostitution. 'Common' also takes in the meanings of 'common land' and 'common law'.

POLLY

Virgins are like the fair flower in its lustre,   10
    Which in the garden enamels the ground;
Near it the bees in play flutter and cluster,
    And gaudy butterflies frolic around.
But when once plucked, 'tis no longer alluring,
    To Covent Garden 'tis sent (as yet sweet),   15
There fades, and shrinks, and grows past all enduring,
    Rots, stinks, and dies, and is trod under feet.

PEACHUM

You know, Polly, I am not against your toying and trifling with
a customer in the way of business, or to get out a secret, or so.
But if I find out that you have played the fool and are married,   20
you jade you, I'll cut your throat, hussy. Now you know my
mind.

9   *Air 6 What . . . Her* opening line of a lyric (by Betterton or Dryden) in the 1690
    adaptation of Beaumont and Fletcher's *The Prophetess: or the History of Dioclesian*
    with music by Purcell. It is a song of adoring love, and Gay's much more bitter lyric
    may specifically be satirising its couplet:
        In Fair *Aurelia*'s Arms leave me expiring,
        To be Embalm'd by the Sweets of her Breath.
15 *Covent Garden* London's main flower market until the 20th century, but also at this
    period an area notorious for prostitution.
21 *jade* Literally an inferior horse, applied insultingly to women.

[ACT I,] SCENE viii

PEACHUM [*and*] POLLY [*remain; to them enter*] MRS PEACHUM

Air 7   Oh London is a Fine Town   [Anon]

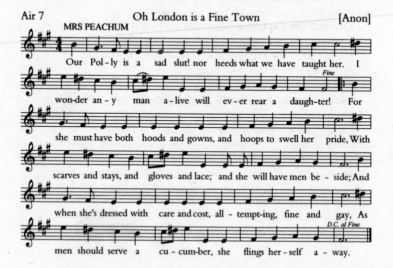

MRS PEACHUM, *in a very great passion*

Our Polly is a sad slut! nor heeds what we have taught her.

I wonder any man alive will ever rear a daughter!

For she must have both hoods and gowns, and hoops to
    swell her pride,

With scarves and stays, and gloves and lace; and she
    will have men beside;

And when she's dressed with care and cost, all-tempting,
    fine and gay,   5

As men should serve a cucumber, she flings herself away.

Our Polly is a sad slut, etc.

---

0 *Air 7 Oh London . . . Town* The dance tune has a long history, under different
    names, and is associated with many ballads. The opening line of Gay's song recalls
    the declarative, descriptive opening to the lyric, which was much parodied.

1 *have* O2; not in O1.

4 *hoops* structures of various shapes, made of whalebone or cane, worn under skirts
    to give them volume. Hooped skirts were fashionable until the 1780s.

5 *stays* corsets.

MRS PEACHUM

You baggage! You hussy! You inconsiderate jade! Had you been hanged, it would not have vexed me, for that might have been your misfortune; but to do such a mad thing by choice! The wench is married, husband. 10

PEACHUM

Married! The Captain is a bold man, and will risk anything for money; to be sure he believes her a fortune. Do you think your mother and I should have lived comfortably so long together, if ever we had been married? Baggage! 15

MRS PEACHUM

I knew she was always a proud slut; and now the wench hath played the fool and married, because forsooth she would do like the gentry. Can you support the expense of a husband, hussy, in gaming, drinking and whoring? Have you money enough to carry on the daily quarrels of man and wife about who shall 20 squander most? There are not many husbands and wives who can bear the charges of plaguing one another in a handsome way. If you must be married, could you introduce nobody into our family but a highwayman? Why, thou foolish jade, thou wilt be as ill-used, and as much neglected, as if thou hadst married a 25 lord!

PEACHUM

Let not your anger, my dear, break through the rules of decency, for the Captain looks upon himself in the military capacity, as a gentleman by his profession. Besides what he hath already, I know he is in a fair way of getting, or of dying; and both these 30 ways, let me tell you, are most excellent chances for a wife. Tell me, hussy, are you ruined or no?

MRS PEACHUM

With Polly's fortune, she might very well have gone off to a person of distinction. Yes, that you might, you pouting slut!

---

6   *As men ... cucumber* Cucumbers were considered to be not worth the time it took to prepare them for eating.

8   *baggage* strumpet, good-for-nothing.
    hussy originally simply 'housewife' (still a live meaning in 1728), but used increasingly as a term of abuse implying an ill-behaved girl.

30 *getting* becoming richer.

32 *ruined* Used here to mean married, rather than with the usual, opposite, sense of a woman losing her virginity outside marriage.

PEACHUM

What, is the wench dumb? Speak, or I'll make you plead by   35
squeezing out an answer from you. Are you really bound wife to
him, or are you only upon liking? (*Pinches her*)

POLLY

(*Screaming*) Oh!

MRS PEACHUM

How the mother is to be pitied who hath handsome daughters!
Lock, bolts, bars, and lectures of morality are nothing to them;   40
they break through them all. They have as much pleasure in
cheating a father and mother as in cheating at cards.

PEACHUM

Why, Polly, I shall soon know if you are married, by Macheath's
keeping from our house.

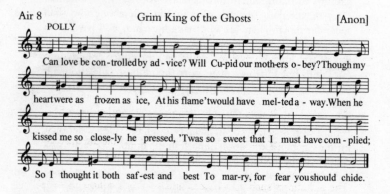

Air 8   Grim King of the Ghosts   [Anon]

Can love be controlled by advice? Will Cupid our mothers obey? Though my heart were as frozen as ice, At his flame 'twould have melted away. When he kissed me so closely he pressed, 'Twas so sweet that I must have complied; So I thought it both safest and best To marry, for fear you should chide.

POLLY

Can love be controlled by advice?   45
    Will Cupid our mothers obey?
Though my heart were as frozen as ice,
    At his flame 'twould have melted away.

When he kissed me so closely he pressed,
    'Twas so sweet that I must have complied;   50

36   *squeezing out an answer* An allusion to 'pressing' or '*peine forte et dure*', the practice
      accepted at the time of torturing, sometimes to death, prisoners who refused to
      enter a plea of guilty or not guilty, by putting heavy weights on their chests.
37   *upon liking* on trial, on approval (*OED, liking* vbln[1], 4c).
44   *Air 8. Grim . . . Ghosts* a widely circulated tune, less miserable than its title suggests.

So I thought it both safest and best
To marry, for fear you should chide.

MRS PEACHUM
Then all the hopes of our family are gone for ever and ever!

PEACHUM
And Macheath may hang his father and mother-in-law, in hope
to get into their daughter's fortune.   55

POLLY
I did not marry him (as 'tis the fashion) coolly and deliberately
for honour or money. But, I love him.

MRS PEACHUM
Love him! Worse and worse! I thought the girl had been better
bred. Oh, husband, husband! Her folly makes me mad!
My head swims! I'm distracted! I can't support myself – Oh!   60
                                                    (*Faints*)

PEACHUM
See, wench, to what a condition you have reduced your poor
mother! A glass of cordial, this instant. How the poor woman
takes it to heart!

POLLY *goes out, and returns with it*

Ah, hussy, this is now the only comfort your mother has left!

POLLY
Give her another glass, sir! My mama drinks double the quantity   65
whenever she is out of order. This, you see, fetches her.

MRS PEACHUM
The girl shows such a readiness, and so much concern, that I
could almost find it in my heart to forgive her.

Air 9   Oh Jenny, Oh Jenny, Where hast thou Been?   [Anon]

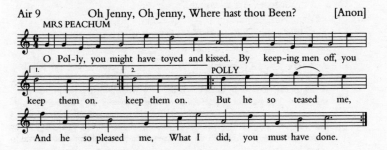

O Pol-ly, you might have toyed and kissed. By keep-ing men off, you
keep them on.   keep them on.   But he so teased me,
And he so pleased me, What I did, you must have done.

66 *fetches* restores to consciousness.

MRS PEACHUM

O Polly, you might have toyed and kissed.
By keeping men off, you keep them on.   70

POLLY

But he so teased me,
And he so pleased me,
What I did, you must have done.

MRS PEACHUM

Not with a highwayman! You sorry slut!

PEACHUM

[*Taking* MRS PEACHUM *aside*] A word with you, wife. 'Tis no   75
new thing for a wench to take a man without consent of parents.
You know 'tis the frailty of woman, my dear.

MRS PEACHUM

Yes, indeed, the sex is frail. But the first time a woman is frail, she
should be somewhat nice methinks, for then or never is the time
to make her fortune. After that, she hath nothing to do but to   80
guard herself from being found out, and she may do what she
pleases.

PEACHUM

Make yourself a little easy; I have a thought shall soon set all
matters again to rights. [*To* POLLY] Why so melancholy, Polly?
Since what is done cannot be undone, we must all endeavour to   85
make the best of it.

MRS PEACHUM

Well, Polly; as far as one woman can forgive another, I forgive
thee. Your father is too fond of you, hussy.

POLLY

Then all my sorrows are at an end.

MRS PEACHUM

A mighty likely speech in troth, for a wench who is just married!   90

---

68   *Air 9 Oh . . . Been* A poem entitled 'A dialogue between two sisters' with this first
     line is found in D'Urfey's *Wit and Mirth: or Pills to Purge Melancholy* (1719–20), 1,
     p. 169, and ascribed to the tune 'The Willoughby Whim', which is not printed with
     the words. The dialogue is a knowing exchange between two women, which, if
     recalled, undercuts Polly's innocence. References to this collection (henceforth
     Pills) are to the six-volume edition of a work which had been enlarged greatly from
     its first publication in 1698. It is a primary source for the identification of Gay's
     tunes.
79   *nice* particular, discriminating.
85   *what . . . undone* Recollecting *Macbeth*, V.i.64.

Air 10   Thomas, I Cannot   [Anon]

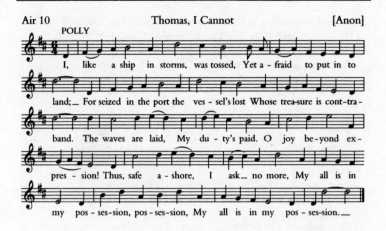

I, like a ship in storms, was tossed, Yet a-fraid to put in to land; — For seized in the port the ves-sel's lost Whose trea-sure is cont-tra-band. The waves are laid, My du-ty's paid. O joy be-yond ex-pres-sion! Thus, safe a-shore, I ask— no more, My all is in my pos-ses-sion, pos-ses-sion, My all is in my pos-ses-sion.—

POLLY

I, like a ship in storms, was tossed,
Yet afraid to put in to land;
For seized in the port the vessel's lost
Whose treasure is contraband.
    The waves are laid,   95
    My duty's paid.
    O joy beyond expression!
    Thus, safe ashore,
    I ask no more,
My all is in my possession.   100

PEACHUM

I hear customers in t'other room; go, talk with 'em, Polly; but
come to us again, as soon as they are gone – but hark ye, child,
if 'tis the gentleman who was here yesterday about the repeating
watch, say you believe we can't get intelligence of it till
tomorrow. For I lent it to Suky Straddle to make a figure with it   105

---

90   *Air 10 Thomas I Cannot* A tune going back at least to the first part of the
      seventeenth century, originally taking its name from the refrain of a ribald song,
      but subsequently set to a wide variety of different verses in broadsides and ballad
      operas. In bar 15 the note on 'more' is C# in O2.

103–4 *gentleman . . . intelligence* Peachum intends to get a reward for returning stolen
      property, once members of his gang have had the benefit of using it.
      repeating watch a watch which struck the quarter hours and could be made to
      repeat the last strike as required.

105 *make a figure* make herself prominent or attractive.

tonight at a tavern in Drury Lane. If t'other gentleman calls for the silver-hilted sword, you know beetle-browed Jemmy hath it on, and he doth not come from Tunbridge till Tuesday night, so that it cannot be had till then.

[*Exit* POLLY]

[ACT I,] SCENE ix

PEACHUM [*and*] MRS PEACHUM [*remain*]

PEACHUM

Dear wife, be a little pacified. Don't let your passion run away with your senses. Polly, I grant you, hath done a rash thing.

MRS PEACHUM

If she had had only an intrigue with the fellow, why, the very best families have excused and huddled up a frailty of that sort. 'Tis marriage, husband, that makes it a blemish.

PEACHUM

But money, wife, is the true fuller's earth for reputations; there is not a spot or a stain but what it can take out. A rich rogue   5
nowadays is fit company for any gentleman; and the world, my dear, hath not such a contempt for roguery as you imagine. I tell you, wife, I can make this match turn to our advantage.

MRS PEACHUM

I am very sensible, husband, that Captain Macheath is worth money, but I am in doubt whether he hath not two or three   10
wives already, and then if he should die in a session or two, Polly's dower would come into a dispute.

PEACHUM

That, indeed, is a point which ought to be considered.

---

106   *Drury Lane* the area north of the Strand and close to Covent Garden, notorious as London's main area for prostitution. Compare Gay's *Trivia*: 'O! may thy virtue guard thee through the roads / Of Drury's mazy courts, and dark abodes, / The harlots guileful paths' (III.259–61).
108   *Tunbridge* Tunbridge Wells, in Kent. A spa town popular with people of fashion.

6   *fuller's earth* a kind of clay used to clean and thicken cloth.
11   *sensible* aware.
14   *dower* the portion of a husband's estate which the law allows to his widow for life.

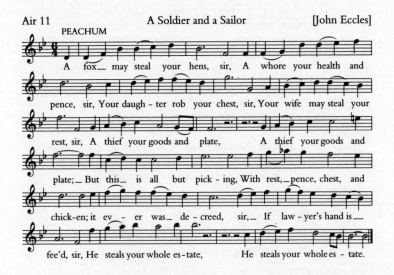

Air 11   A Soldier and a Sailor   [John Eccles]

PEACHUM

A fox— may steal your hens, sir, A whore your health and pence, sir, Your daugh-ter rob your chest, sir, Your wife may steal your rest, sir, A thief your goods and plate, A thief your goods and plate;— But this— is all but pick-ing, With rest,— pence, chest, and chick-en; it ev – er was— de-creed, sir, If law-yer's hand is— fee'd, sir, He steals your whole es-tate, He steals your whole es – tate.

PEACHUM   15

> A fox may steal your hens, sir,
> A whore your health and pence, sir,
> Your daughter rob your chest, sir,
> Your wife may steal your rest, sir,
>   A thief your goods and plate;
> But this is all but picking,
> With rest, pence, chest and chicken;
> It ever was decreed, sir,   20
> If lawyer's hand is fee'd, sir,
>   He steals your whole estate.

PEACHUM

The lawyers are bitter enemies to those in our way. They don't   25
care that anybody should get a clandestine livelihood but
themselves.

---

15   *Air 11 A . . . Sailor* A lyric and tune which originated as a dialogue song in
Congreve's *Love for Love* (1695), with music by John Eccles. Unlike other
ballads to this tune, Gay's does not adopt the dialogue structure. The tune
was printed a fourth lower in the first two editions.
21   *picking* petty theft.

[ACT I,] SCENE x

MRS PEACHUM [*and*] PEACHUM [*remain; to them enter*] POLLY

POLLY

'Twas only Nimming Ned. He brought in a damask window-curtain, a hoop-petticoat, a pair of silver candlesticks, and one silk stocking, from the fire that happened last night.

PEACHUM

There is not a fellow that is cleverer in his way, and saves more goods out of the fire than Ned. But now, Polly, to your affair, for 5 matters must not be left as they are. You are married, then, it seems?

POLLY

Yes, sir.

PEACHUM

And how do you propose to live, child?

POLLY

Like other women, sir, upon the industry of my husband. 10

MRS PEACHUM

What, is the wench turned fool? A highwayman's wife, like a soldier's, hath as little of his pay as of his company.

PEACHUM

And had not you the common views of a gentlewoman in your marriage, Polly?

POLLY

I don't know what you mean, sir. 15

PEACHUM

Of a jointure, and of being a widow.

POLLY

But I love him, sir; how then could I have thoughts of parting with him?

PEACHUM

Parting with him! Why, that is the whole scheme and intention of all marriage articles. The comfortable estate of widowhood 20 is the only hope that keeps up a wife's spirits. Where is the woman who would scruple to be a wife, if she had it in her

---

1 *damask* richly patterned fabric.

16 *jointure* property either held jointly by a husband and wife or legally designated for the wife's sole use in the event of her husband's death. In either case, the intention was to make provision for widows.

power to be a widow whenever she pleased? If you have any
views of this sort, Polly, I shall think the match not so very
unreasonable.   25

POLLY

How I dread to hear your advice! Yet I must beg you to explain
yourself.

PEACHUM

Secure what he hath got, have him peached the next sessions,
and then at once you are made a rich widow.

POLLY

What, murder the man I love? The blood runs cold at my heart   30
with the very thought of it!

PEACHUM

Fie, Polly! What hath murder to do in the affair? Since the thing
sooner or later must happen, I dare say the Captain himself
would like that we should get the reward for his death sooner
than a stranger. Why, Polly, the Captain knows that as 'tis his   35
employment to rob, so 'tis ours to take robbers. Every man in his
business. So there is no malice in the case.

MRS PEACHUM

Ay, husband, now you have nicked the matter. To have him
peached is the only thing could ever make me forgive her.

Air 12   Now Ponder Well, ye Parents Dear   [Anon]

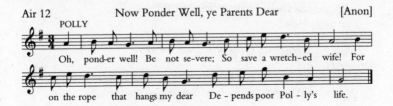

POLLY

Oh, ponder well! Be not severe;   40
So save a wretched wife!
For on the rope that hangs my dear
Depends poor Polly's life.

28   *peached* informed against.
38   *nicked the matter* grasped or hit on the situation precisely.
39   *Air 12 Now . . . Dear* This is the first line of an enormously popular ballad dating
     from 1595, telling the story of two children abandoned to die in a wood. Gay takes
     over the melancholy associations the tune carried, and uses them without irony.
     Barlow gives strong evidence that the song was sung twice, perhaps addressed first

MRS PEACHUM

But your duty to your parents, hussy, obliges you to hang him.
What would many a wife give for such an opportunity! 45

POLLY

What is a jointure, what is widowhood to me? I know my heart.
I cannot survive him.

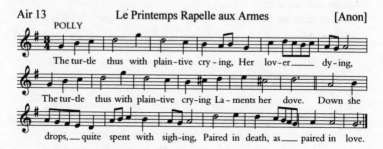

Air 13　　　　　Le Printemps Rapelle aux Armes　　　　[Anon]

POLLY

The turtle thus with plaintive crying,
　　　Her lover dying,
The turtle thus with plaintive crying 50
　　　Laments her dove.
Down she drops, quite spent with sighing,
Paired in death, as paired in love.

POLLY

Thus, sir, it will happen to your poor Polly.

MRS PEACHUM

What, is the fool in love in earnest then? I hate thee for being 55
particular. Why, wench, thou art a shame to thy very sex.

to her mother, then her father. This was the song which was said to spark positive
audience reaction on the first night.

43　*Depends* a pun for an audience in the eighteenth century when 'to depend' could also
mean 'to hang down'.

47　*Air 13 Le . . . Armes* one of four French tunes in the opera. A version close to that
used here appears in *The Bird Fancyer's Delight* (1717), a collection of tunes for solo
recorder or flute to teach caged birds to sing. Gay is reputed to have been a flautist,
and may well have known the tune by this route. The French words are spoken by a
woman plunged into melancholy by the departure of her soldier lover.

48　*turtle* turtledove; traditionally associated with marital affection and constancy.

56　*particular* exclusively committed to one person, but also 'odd', 'strange'.

POLLY
But hear me, mother. If you ever loved –

MRS PEACHUM
Those cursed playbooks she reads have been her ruin. One word more, hussy, and I shall knock your brains out, if you have any.

PEACHUM
Keep out of the way, Polly, for fear of mischief, and consider of   60
what is proposed to you.

MRS PEACHUM
Away, hussy! Hang your husband, and be dutiful!

POLLY [*appears to leave, but stays*] *listening*

[ACT I,] SCENE xi

MRS PEACHUM [*and*] PEACHUM [*remain,
with* POLLY *overhearing*]

MRS PEACHUM
The thing, husband, must and shall be done. For the sake of intelligence we must take other measures, and have him peached the next session without her consent. If she will not know her duty, we know ours.

PEACHUM
But really, my dear, it grieves one's heart to take off a great man.   5
When I consider his personal bravery, his fine stratagem, how much we have already got by him, and how much more we may get, methinks I can't find it in my heart to have a hand in his death. I wish you could have made Polly undertake it.

MRS PEACHUM
But in a case of necessity – our own lives are in danger.   10

PEACHUM
Then, indeed, we must comply with the customs of the world, and make gratitude give way to interest. He shall be taken off.

---

58   *Those cursed playbooks she reads* Reading plays and romances was often cited by moralists and educationists as having a dangerous effect on the social and romantic aspirations of young women.

1–2   *For the sake of intelligence* i.e. because Macheath has information which could incriminate them.

6   *stratagem* ingenuity, cunning.

MRS PEACHUM
> I'll undertake to manage Polly.

PEACHUM
> And I'll prepare matters for the Old Bailey.

> > [*Exeunt* PEACHUM, MRS PEACHUM]

[ACT I,] SCENE xii

POLLY [*remains, alone*]

POLLY
> Now I'm a wretch, indeed. – Methinks I see him already in the
> cart, sweeter and more lovely than the nosegay in his hand! – I
> hear the crowd extolling his resolution and intrepidity! – What
> volleys of sighs are sent from the windows of Holborn, that so
> comely a youth should be brought to disgrace! – I see him at the   5
> tree! The whole circle are in tears! – Even butchers weep! Jack
> Ketch himself hesitates to perform his duty, and would be glad
> to lose his fee by a reprieve. What then will become of Polly? –
> As yet I may inform him of their design, and aid him in his
> escape. – It shall be so. – But then he flies, absents himself, and I   10
> bar myself from his dear, dear conversation! That too will
> distract me. – If he keep out of the way, my papa and mama may
> in time relent, and we may be happy. If he stays, he is hanged,

1–12   *Now I'm a wretch . . . will distract me* Polly's speech burlesques the inflated
emotional language of contemporary sentimental drama, in particular the popular
'she-tragedies' such as *The Fair Penitent* (1703) and *Lady Jane Grey* (1715) by the
Whig playwright and poet laureate Nicholas Rowe (1674–1718). Like all good
mock-heroic writing, it achieves a complex balance of comedy and pathos. The use
of long dashes to indicate the syntactic turns and pauses of extreme emotion was
conventional in the period.

1–6   *in the cart . . . nosegay . . . Holborn . . . the tree* Condemned prisoners were taken
from Newgate to their execution in an open cart, watched, jeered and supported by
huge crowds. At the church of St Sepulchre, near Newgate, friends handed the
prisoners nosegays of coloured flowers. The route to 'Tyburn Tree' (the gallows) at
Tyburn (near the modern Marble Arch) passed along Holborn and Tyburn Road
(now Oxford Street).

6   *butchers* The Theatre Royal in Lincoln's Inn Fields, where the first performance was
staged, was next to Clare Market, whose butchers were amongst its supporters.

6–7   *Jack Ketch* public hangman who died in 1686. The name became synonymous with
the role of public executioner.

11   *conversation* used at this period to mean sexual as well as social intercourse.

and then he is lost for ever! – He intended to lie concealed in my
room till the dusk of the evening; if they are abroad, I'll this   15
instant let him out, lest some accident should prevent him.

Exit[s], and returns [with MACHEATH]

[ACT I,] SCENE xiii

POLLY [*and*] MACHEATH

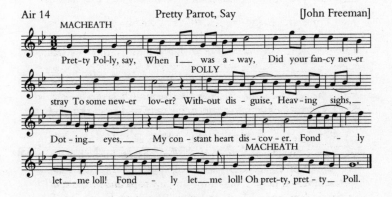

Air 14   Pretty Parrot, Say   [John Freeman]

MACHEATH
Pret-ty Pol-ly, say, When I__ was a-way, Did your fan-cy nev-er

POLLY
stray To some new-er lov-er? With-out dis - guise, Heav-ing sighs,__

Dot-ing__ eyes,__ My con - stant heart dis-cov-er. Fond - ly

MACHEATH
let__me loll! Fond - ly let__me loll! Oh pret-ty, pret-ty__ Poll.

MACHEATH
Pretty Polly, say,
When I was away,
Did your fancy never stray
To some newer lover?
POLLY
Without disguise,   5
Heaving sighs,
Doting eyes,
My constant heart discover.
Fondly let me loll!

0   *Air 14 Pretty . . . Say* The tune is named after a translation from the French, first
published in 1706, beginning 'Pretty parrot, say, when I was away'. This lyric suggests
that the 'pretty parrot' was indeed unfaithful, and though Gay redirects the song
through Polly's declaration of constancy, the resonances of the original clearly inten-
sify Macheath's suspicious opening. This song in turn spawned a number of parodies.

MACHEATH

O pretty, pretty Poll.   10

POLLY

And are *you* as fond as ever, my dear?

MACHEATH

Suspect my honour, my courage, suspect any thing but my love.
May my pistols misfire, and my mare slip her shoulder while I
am pursued, if I ever forsake thee!

POLLY

Nay, my dear, I have no reason to doubt you, for I find in the   15
romance you lent me, none of the great heroes were ever false in
love.

Air 15   Pray, Fair One, be Kind   [Richard Leveridge]

MACHEATH

My heart was so free,
It roved like the bee,
Till Polly my passion requited;   20
I sipped each flower,
I changed ev'ry hour,
But here ev'ry flower is united.

Charlot & the Dulce,
New Atalantis

15–16 *the romance you lent me* See note to I.x.58. A tantalising insight into Macheath's
means of seduction: sharing, but also perhaps manipulating, Polly's upwardly
mobile literary tastes.

17   *Air 15 Pray . . . Kind* A song by Leveridge originating in Farquhar's *The Recruiting
Officer*, Act 3 (though cut in later editions of the play), where it is described as a
'rough military air'. Its singer protests that he is not interested in his beloved for her
money. Gay only uses the first musical section of the much longer song. In the final
bar the text in the music of Q1 reads 'Flower's'.

POLLY

Were you sentenced to transportation, sure, my dear, you could
not leave me behind you – could you?   25

MACHEATH

Is there any power, any force that could tear me from thee?
You might sooner tear a pension out of the hands of a courtier,
a fee from a lawyer, a pretty woman from a looking-glass, or
any woman from quadrille – but to tear me from thee is
impossible!   30

Air 16   Over the Hills and Far Away   [Anon]

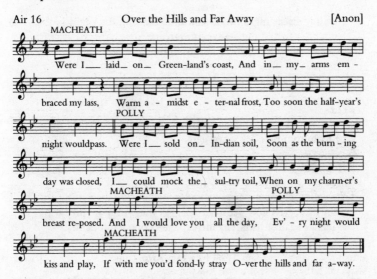

MACHEATH
Were I laid on Greenland's coast,
And in my arms embraced my lass,

27 *pension* regular payment. Here specifically implying that given to a courtier to buy
    their allegiance to a particular faction. Johnson's *Dictionary* (1755) defined
    'pension' as 'pay given to a state hireling for treason to his country'.

30 *Air 16 Over . . . Away* A tune with a number of potential resonances for the original
    audience. The name comes from the refrain of a song entitled 'Jockey's
    Lamentation' first printed in 1706. The song tells of Jenny's desertion of her lover,
    which might undercut the togetherness Macheath and Polly protest. The tune also
    sets a lyric in Farquhar's *The Recruiting Officer* enticing potential recruits with the
    possibility of escaping domesticity, and it is associated with a number of songs
    both pro- and anti- James Stuart, the 'Pretender', as well as with a ballad 'Hubble
    Bubbles' concerning the stock market crash known as the 'South Sea Bubble'.

Warm amidst eternal frost,
Too soon the half-year's night would pass.

POLLY

Were I sold on Indian soil,   35
Soon as the burning day was closed,
I could mock the sultry toil,
When on my charmer's breast reposed.

MACHEATH

And I would love you all the day,

POLLY

Every night would kiss and play,   40

MACHEATH

If with me you'd fondly stray

POLLY

Over the hills and far away.

POLLY

Yes, I would go with thee. But oh! How shall I speak it? I must
be torn from thee. We must part.

MACHEATH

How? Part?   45

POLLY

We must, we must. My papa and mama are set against thy life.
They now, even now, are in search after thee. They are preparing
evidence against thee. Thy life depends upon a moment.

Air 17   Gin Thou wert min Awn Thing   [Anon]

48   *Air 17 Gin . . . Thing* The title comes from the first line of a lyric entitled 'A Scotch
Song' first printed on a song sheet in 1710. Gay's tune is not very close to this original.

38

POLLY

Oh, what pain it is to part!
Can I leave thee, can I leave thee?   50
Oh, what pain it is to part!
Can thy Polly ever leave thee?
But lest death my love should thwart,
And bring thee to the fatal cart,
Thus I tear thee from my bleeding heart!   55
Fly hence, and let me leave thee.

POLLY

One kiss and then – one kiss – begone – farewell.

MACHEATH

My hand, my heart, my dear, is so riveted to thine that I cannot
unloose my hold.

POLLY

But my papa may intercept thee, and then I should lose the very   60
glimmering of hope. A few weeks, perhaps, may reconcile us all.
Shall thy Polly hear from thee?

MACHEATH

Must I then go?

POLLY

And will not absence change your love?

MACHEATH

If you doubt it, let me stay – and be hanged.   65

POLLY

Oh, how I fear, how I tremble! Go! But when safety will give you
leave, you will be sure to see me again; for till then Polly is wretched.

Air 18   Oh, the Broom   [Anon]

MACHEATH The mi – ser thus   a   shil – ling__ sees   Which
POLLY   The boy,   thus, when   his spar – row's flown, The__

he's ob – liged__ to__ pay;   With sighs__ re – signs__ it__
bird in__ si – lence__ eyes;   But soon__ as__ out__ of__

by   de – grees,   And fears 'tis__ gone__ for__ aye.
sight 'tis__ gone, Whines, whim – pers,__ sobs,__ and__ cries.

39

[*They sing while*] *parting, and looking back at each other
with fondness; he at one door, she at the other*

MACHEATH

The miser thus a shilling sees
   Which he's obliged to pay;
With sighs resigns it by degrees,   70
   And fears 'tis gone for aye.

POLLY

The boy, thus, when his sparrow's flown,
   The bird in silence eyes;
But soon as out of sight 'tis gone,
   Whines, whimpers, sobs and cries.   75

[*Exeunt*]

66   *Air 18 Oh the Broom* a tune with a long history, and attached to many ballads. The version here is more elaborate than others, its dotted rhythms perhaps emphasising the fact that it was (probably wrongly) identified as a Scottish tune. Printed in E-flat in O1 and 2, with some minor rhythmic and melodic differences.

ACT II, SCENE i

[Scene,] a tavern near Newgate

JEMMY TWITCHER, CROOK-FINGERED JACK,
WAT DREARY, ROBIN OF BAGSHOT, NIMMING NED,
HARRY PADINGTON, MATT OF THE MINT, BEN BUDGE,
and the rest of the gang at the table, with wine, brandy, and tobacco

BEN BUDGE
But prithee, Matt, what is become of thy brother Tom? I have
not seen him since my return from transportation.

MATT OF THE MINT
Poor brother Tom had an accident this time twelvemonth, and
so clever a made fellow he was, that I could not save him from
those flaying rascals the surgeons; and now, poor man, he is   5
among the ottomies at Surgeons' Hall.

BEN BUDGE
So, it seems, his time was come.

JEMMY TWITCHER
But the present time is ours, and nobody alive hath more. Why
are the laws levelled at us? Are we more dishonest than the rest
of mankind? What we win, gentlemen, is our own by the law of   10
arms, and the right of conquest.

CROOK-FINGERED JACK
Where shall we find such another set of practical philosophers,
who to a man are above the fear of death?

WAT DREARY
Sound men, and true!

ROBIN OF BAGSHOT
Of tried courage and indefatigable industry!   15

NIMMING NED
Who is there here that would not die for his friend?

---

0   s.d. 3 *HARRY* ed. Here, and at 18 below, O1, O2 and Q1 have *HENRY*. There seems
    no reason to preserve the anomaly.
4   *so clever a made* so well-made, well-formed (that he was attractive to the surgeons).
5–6 *flaying rascals . . . Surgeons' Hall* The bodies of executed criminals were used for
    dissection in the anatomy demonstrations held at the Barber-Surgeons' Hall in
    Monkwell Square in the City of London, and their skeletons ('ottomies', or
    'anatomies') were then put on display.

HARRY PADDINGTON

Who is there here that would betray him for his interest?

MATT OF THE MINT

Show me a gang of courtiers that can say as much.

BEN BUDGE

We are for a just partition of the world, for every man hath a
right to enjoy life.   20

MATT OF THE MINT

We retrench the superfluities of mankind. The world is
avaricious, and I hate avarice. A covetous fellow, like a jackdaw,
steals what he was never made to enjoy, for the sake of hiding
it. These are the robbers of mankind, for money was made
for the free-hearted and generous, and where is the injury   25
of taking from another what he hath not the heart to make use
of?

JEMMY TWITCHER

Our several stations for the day are fixed. Good luck attend us
all. Fill the glasses!

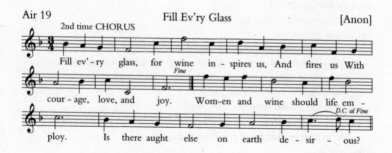

Air 19   Fill Ev'ry Glass   [Anon]

2nd time CHORUS

Fill ev'-ry glass, for wine in-spires us, And fires us With
cour-age, love, and joy. Wom-en and wine should life employ. Is there aught else on earth de-sir-ous?

Fine

D.C. al Fine

MATT OF THE MINT

Fill ev'ry glass, for wine inspires us,   30
        And fires us
With courage, love, and joy.
Women and wine should life employ.
Is there aught else on earth desirous?

CHORUS

Fill ev'ry Glass, etc.   35

23   *jackdaw* a member of the crow family, traditionally associated with stealing.
29   *Air 19 Fill Ev'ry Glass* The tune's title is taken from the first line of a drinking song,
     'In praise of our three famed generals', D'Urfey's translation of a French text. The

42

[ACT II,] SCENE ii

To them enter MACHEATH

MACHEATH

Gentlemen, well met. My heart hath been with you this hour, but an unexpected affair hath detained me. No ceremony, I beg you.

MATT OF THE MINT

We were just breaking up to go upon duty. Am I to have the honour of taking the air with you, sir, this evening upon the heath? I drink a dram now and then with the stage-coachmen in the way of friendship and intelligence, and I know that about this time there will be passengers upon the western road who are worth speaking with.

MACHEATH

I was to have been of that party – but –

MATT OF THE MINT

But what, sir?

MACHEATH

Is there any man who suspects my courage?

MATT OF THE MINT

We have all been witnesses of it.

MACHEATH

My honour and truth to the gang?

MATT OF THE MINT

I'll be answerable for it.

MACHEATH

In the division of our booty have I ever shown the least marks of avarice or injustice?

French tune is still known today in carols such as 'Whence is that goodly fragrance'. There are a number of ways of performing the song; it is often repeated several times in performance.

2 *No ceremony* Macheath either responds to some gesture by the others – a salute or a bow, or the fact that they rise to their feet – or else he speaks ironically as the thieves are about to leave.

5–6 *taking the air . . . upon the heath* The language of politeness is euphemistically used to describe a highway robbery expedition.

8 *western road* The Bath and Exeter road west out of London ran across Hounslow Heath, one of the most dangerous haunts of highwaymen.

MATT OF THE MINT

By these questions something seems to have ruffled you. Are any of us suspected?

MACHEATH

I have a fixed confidence, gentlemen, in you all as men of honour, and as such I value and respect you. Peachum is a man that is useful to us.

MATT OF THE MINT

Is he about to play us any foul play? I'll shoot him through the head.

MACHEATH

I beg you, gentlemen, act with conduct and discretion. A pistol is your last resort.

MATT OF THE MINT

He knows nothing of this meeting.

MACHEATH

Business cannot go on without him. He is a man who knows the world, and is a necessary agent to us. We have had a slight difference, and till it is accommodated I shall be obliged to keep out of his way. Any private dispute of mine shall be of no ill consequence to my friends. You must continue to act under his direction, for the moment we break loose from him, our gang is ruined.

MATT OF THE MINT

As a bawd to a whore, I grant you, he is to us of great convenience.

MACHEATH

Make him believe I have quitted the gang, which I can never do but with life. At our private quarters I will continue to meet you. A week or so will probably reconcile us.

MATT OF THE MINT

Your instructions shall be observed. 'Tis now high time for us to repair to our several duties; so till the evening at our quarters in Moorfields we bid you farewell.

MACHEATH

I shall wish myself with you. Success attend you.

Sits down melancholy at the table

25   *conduct* (1) skill, tact (*OED* conduct n.1, 7) or (2) moral principle (*OED* 8).
35   *bawd* female brothel-keeper or procuress.
41   *several* separate, particular.
42   *Moorfields* an area north of the City of London associated with criminality.

Air 20   March in *Rinaldo* with Drums and Trumpets   [Handel]

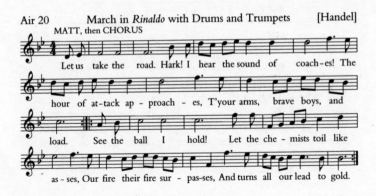

MATT, then CHORUS

Let us take the road. Hark! I hear the sound of coach-es! The hour of at-tack ap - proach - es, T'your arms, brave boys, and load. See the ball I hold! Let the che - mists toil like as - ses, Our fire their fire sur - pas-ses, And turns all our lead to gold.

MATT OF THE MINT

Let us take the road.
 Hark! I hear the sound of coaches!   45
 The hour of attack approaches,
T'your arms, brave boys, and load.
 See the ball I hold!
 Let the chemists toil like asses,
 Our fire their fire surpasses,   50
  And turns all our lead to gold.

*The gang, ranged in the front of the stage, load their pistols,
and stick them under their girdles; then go off singing
the first part in chorus*

43 *Air 20 March in Rinaldo* Tune from George Frideric Handel's first opera for
 the English stage, (1711). In its original setting it is purely instrumental,
 scored for four trumpets, timpani, oboes and strings. It had already been
 appropriated for a tavern song 'Let the waiter bring clean glasses'. The tune,
 in exactly the form Gay uses, is also found in *The Bird Fancyer's Delight* (see
 note to I.x.47).

47 *T'your* As Q1 music. The elision is not present in the texts, which give 'To
 your', but it is required by the music.

48–51 *See the . . . gold* The conceit compares highwaymen favourably with
 alchemists on the grounds that their pistol fire is more successful than the
 fire of the alchemists' experiments in turning lead (bullets, or 'ball') into
 gold.

[ACT II,] SCENE iii

MACHEATH [*remains, alone*]

MACHEATH

What a fool is a fond wench! Polly is most confoundedly bit. –
I love the sex. And a man who loves money might as well be
contented with one guinea, as I with one woman. The town
perhaps hath been as much obliged to me for recruiting it with
free-hearted ladies, as to any recruiting officer in the army. If it   5
were not for us, and the other gentlemen of the sword, Drury-
Lane would be uninhabited.

Air 21   Would you have a Young Virgin   [Thomas D'Urfey]

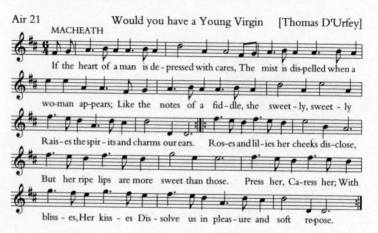

MACHEATH

If the heart of a man is depressed with cares,
The mist is dispelled when a woman appears;
Like the notes of a fiddle, she sweetly, sweetly   10
Raises the spirits and charms our ears.

0   s.d. *alone* ed. The Drawer is listed here in the original editions, but clearly enters later.
1   *bit* bitten by love, but also deceived by Macheath.
3   *guinea* coin worth 21 shillings, or one pound and one shilling (105 pence in today's
    UK currency).
4–6 *recruiting . . . sword* a cynical justification for male promiscuity found in much
    libertine literature of the period. The innocent young women seduced and then
    abandoned have no alternative but to join London's 'army' of prostitutes.
    Macheath identifies himself with army officers, thus suggesting that this treatment
    of women is not confined to the criminal classes.

Roses and lilies her cheeks disclose,
But her ripe lips are more sweet than those.
  Press her,
  Caress her;   15
  With blisses,
  Her kisses
Dissolve us in pleasure and soft repose.

MACHEATH

I must have women. There is nothing unbends the mind like
them. Money is not so strong a cordial for the time. Drawer! 20

     Enter DRAWER

Is the porter gone for all the ladies according to my directions?

DRAWER

I expect him back every minute. But you know, sir, you sent him
as far as Hockley in the Hole for three of the ladies, for one in
Vinegar Yard and for the rest of them somewhere about
Lewkner's Lane. Sure some of them are below, for I hear the bar 25
bell. As they come I will show them up. [*Shouts*] Coming,
Coming!   [*Exit*]

[ACT II,] SCENE iv

MACHEATH [*remains; enter to him in turn*] MRS COAXER,
DOLLY TRULL, MRS VIXEN, BETTY DOXY, JENNY DIVER,
MRS SLAMMEKIN, SUKY TAWDRY, AND MOLLY BRAZEN.

MACHEATH

Dear Mrs Coaxer, you are welcome. You look charmingly
today. I hope you don't want the repairs of quality, and lay on
paint. – Dolly Trull! Kiss me, you slut; are you as amorous as

 7 *Air 21 Would ... Virgin* In D'Urfey's *Songs Compleat* (1719, p. 132) it is described
   as 'A song in the last act of *The Modern Prophets*.' The play was first performed and
   printed in 1709. Its lyrics are even more cynical than Macheath's are here, describ-
   ing the tactics of a man wooing successively a 15-year-old virgin, a widow and a
   prostitute to ensure that 'all's your own'.
 20 *Money ... time* Even money is not such a powerful source of comfort in hard times.
 24–5 *Vinegar Yard ... Lewkner's Lane* near Drury Lane; haunts of prostitutes. Jonathan
   Wild (see Introduction pp. xiii–xv) ran a brothel in Lewkner's Lane.

ever, hussy? You are always so taken up with stealing hearts
that you don't allow yourself time to steal anything else. – Ah 5
Dolly, thou wilt ever be a coquette! – Mrs Vixen, I'm yours. I
always loved a woman of wit and spirit; they make charming
mistresses, but plaguy wives. – Betty Doxy! Come hither, hussy.
Do you drink as hard as ever? You had better stick to good
wholesome beer, for in troth, Betty, strong waters will in time 10
ruin your constitution. You should leave those to your betters. –
What! And my pretty Jenny Diver too! As prim and demure
as ever! There is not any prude, though ever so high-bred,
hath a more sanctified look with a more mischievous heart.
Ah! Thou art a dear artful hypocrite. – Mrs Slammekin! As 15
careless and genteel as ever! All you fine ladies, who know your
own beauty, affect an undress. – But see, here's Suky Tawdry
come to contradict what I am saying. Everything she gets one
way she lays out upon her back. Why, Suky, you must keep
at least a dozen tallymen. Molly Brazen! (*She kisses him.*) That's 20
well done. I love a free-hearted wench. Thou hast a most
agreeable assurance, girl, and art as willing as a turtle. [*Offstage
music*] But hark! I hear music. The harper is at the door. 'If
music be the food of love, play on.' Ere you seat yourselves,
ladies, what think you of a dance? Come in! 25

1–20 The dashes in this speech mark Macheath's turning to each of the women, but also
perhaps imply some stage business as he greets them one by one. In recent
performances this business is often extended.

2 *I hope . . . quality* i.e. I hope you're not lacking the means which women of quality
use to improve their looks.

3 *paint* cosmetics. 6 *a coquette* a flirt.

10 *good wholesome beer . . . strong waters* Beer was a standard drink, even for children,
and thought to be beneficial to health, whereas spirits, particularly gin, were
associated with decay and social disorder.

16–17 *careless . . . an undress* 'Undress' for fashionable women was non-formal dress or
'dishabille', associated with morning wear; Macheath's praise for Mrs Slammekin's
'genteel' carelessness draws ironic attention to her sluttish appearance.

18–19 *Everything . . . upon her back* i.e. she spends all the money she earns through prostitution on clothes; there is an obvious bawdy double entendre in 'upon her back'.

20 *tallymen* tradesmen who provide goods on credit – particularly, here, clothes to
prostitutes.

22 *turtle* turtledove. See note to I.x.48

23 *harper* Itinerant Irish harpists, playing a simple and portable form of the
instrument (still known as an Irish harp), were to be found in London. The harpist
is not mentioned in the cast list, and no music is given for him to play before his
entrance. He may have been casually employed. Roger Fiske, *English Theatre Music
in the Eighteenth Century* (1986) p. 118, notes that the harpist was always dropped
from late-eighteenth-century performances.

Enter HARPER

Play the French tune that Mrs Slammekin was so fond of.

A dance a la ronde in the French manner;
near the end of it this song and chorus.

Air 22   Cotillon   [Anon]

MACHEATH

Youth's the season made for joys;
    Love is then our duty;
She alone who that employs,
    Well deserves her beauty.   30

23–4   *'If music . . . play on'* the first line of Shakespeare's *Twelfth Night*, spoken by the love-sick Duke Orsino.

26   s.d. *dance a la ronde . . . French manner* The dances at formal balls and assemblies at this period were English and French country dances, performed either in a set of couples facing each other or, as here, in a circle. Formal dances were also included in Italian opera. Macheath and the prostitutes again burlesque the activities of polite society.

Air 22 Cotillon or 'cotillion', a term used to describe several French country dances. The word may derive from the second line of the French song to this tune: 'Ma commère quand je danse, / mon cotillon va-t-il bien'. (A 'cotillon' is, originally, an under-petticoat.)

> Let's be gay
>   While we may;
> Beauty's a flower, despised in decay.
>   [CHORUS]
> Youth's the season etc.
>   [MACHEATH]
> Let us drink and sport today;   35
>   Ours is not tomorrow.
> Love with youth flies swift away,
>   Age is nought but sorrow.
>   Dance and sing,
>   Time's on the wing;   40
> Life never knows the return of spring.
>   [CHORUS]
> Let us drink, etc.

MACHEATH

Now, pray ladies, take your places. Here fellow. (*Pays the* HARPER) Bid the drawer bring us more wine.

Exit HARPER

If any of the ladies choose gin, I hope they will be so free to call   45
for it.

JENNY DIVER

You look as if you meant me. Wine is strong enough for me. Indeed, sir, I never drink strong waters, but when I have the colic.

MACHEATH

Just the excuse of the fine ladies! Why, a lady of quality is never   50
without the colic. I hope, Mrs Coaxer, you have had good success of late in your visits among the mercers.

MRS COAXER

We have so many interlopers. Yet with industry one may still have a little picking. I carried a silver-flowered lute-string and a piece of black paduasoy to Mr Peachum's lock but last week.   55

MRS VIXEN

There's Molly Brazen hath the ogle of a rattlesnake. She riveted

---

49   *colic* stomach-ache.
52   *mercers* sellers of fine cloth.
54   *lute-string* 'A kind of glossy silk fabric' (*OED*).
55   *paduasoy* 'A strong, rich, silk fabric, usually slightly corded or embossed' (*OED*).
56   *ogle of a rattlesnake* an ogle is an amorous or lecherous glance or look. Rattlesnakes were commonly believed to fix their prey by gazing at them.

a linen-draper's eye so fast upon her, that he was nicked of three pieces of cambric before he could look off.

MOLLY BRAZEN

Oh dear madam! But sure nothing can come up to your handling of laces! And then you have such a sweet deluding tongue! To cheat a man is nothing; but the woman must have fine parts indeed who cheats a woman! 60

MRS VIXEN

Lace, madam, lies in a small compass, and is of easy conveyance. But you are apt, madam, to think too well of your friends. 65

MRS COAXER

If any woman hath more art than another, to be sure, 'tis Jenny Diver. Though her fellow be never so agreeable, she can pick his pocket as coolly as if money were her only pleasure. Now that is a command of the passions uncommon in a woman!

JENNY DIVER

I never go to the tavern with a man but in the view of business. 70 I have other hours, and other sort of men for my pleasure. But had I your address, madam –

MACHEATH

Have done with your compliments, ladies, and drink about. [*To* JENNY] You are not so fond of me, Jenny, as you use to be.

JENNY DIVER

'Tis not convenient, sir, to show my fondness among so many 75 rivals. 'Tis your own choice, and not the warmth of my inclination, that will determine you.

Air 23   All in a Misty Morning   [Anon]

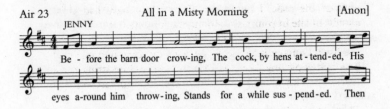

JENNY

Be - fore the barn door crow-ing, The cock, by hens at - tend-ed, His eyes a-round him throw-ing, Stands for a while sus - pend-ed. Then

---

62   *parts* abilities, talents.
72   *address* skill, dexterity, adroitness (*OED* I.4).
77   *determine you* make you decide, come to a resolution.
77   *Air 23 All . . . Morning.* The tune, which dates back at least to the seventeenth century, has various names. The version here alludes to the first line of a narrative

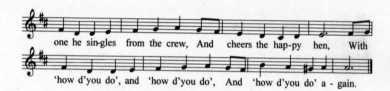

one he sin-gles from the crew, And cheers the hap-py hen, With

'how d'you do', and 'how d'you do', And 'how d'you do' a - gain.

JENNY DIVER

Before the barn door crowing,
    The cock, by hens attended,
His eyes around him throwing,   80
    Stands for a while suspended.
Then one he singles from the crew,
    And cheers the happy hen,
With 'how d'you do', and 'how d'you do',
    And 'how d'you do' again.   85

MACHEATH

Ah Jenny! Thou art a dear slut.

DOLLY TRULL

[*To* SUKY TAWDRY] Pray, madam, were you ever in keeping?

SUKY TAWDRY

I hope, madam, I han't been so long upon the town, but I have
met with some good fortune as well as my neighbours.   90

DOLLY TRULL

Pardon me, madam, I meant no harm by the question; 'twas
only in the way of conversation.

SUKY TAWDRY

Indeed, madam, if I had not been a fool, I might have lived very
handsomely with my last friend. But upon his missing five
guineas, he turned me off. Now I never suspected he had   95
counted them.

MRS SLAMMEKIN

Who do you look upon, madam, as your best sort of keepers?

DOLLY TRULL

That, madam, is thereafter as they be.

of rural wooing, in which each stanza has the 'how d'you do' refrain. Barlow ed., p.
85, persuasively suggests that the key signature should be three sharps (A major),
rather than the two sharps (D major) of all the original texts.
87–8   *in keeping* kept as a mistress.
  98   *thereafter . . . be* according to the way they subsequently behave.

MRS SLAMMEKIN

I, madam, was once kept by a Jew; and, bating their religion, to
women they are a good sort of people.   100

SUKY TAWDRY

Now for my part, I own I like an old fellow, for we always make
them pay for what they can't do.

MRS VIXEN

A spruce prentice, let me tell you, ladies, is no ill thing; they
bleed freely. I have sent at least two or three dozen of them in my
time to the plantations.   105

JENNY DIVER

But to be sure, sir, with so much good fortune as you have had
upon the road, you must be grown immensely rich.

MACHEATH

The road, indeed, hath done me justice, but the gaming table
hath been my ruin.

Air 24   When Once I Lay with Another Man's Wife   [Anon]

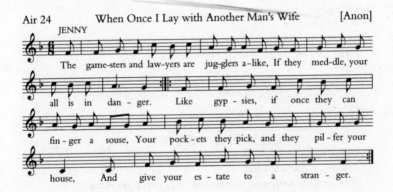

The game-sters and law-yers are jug-glers a-like, If they med-dle, your
all is in dan-ger. Like gyp-sies, if once they can
fin-ger a souse, Your pock-ets they pick, and they pil-fer your
house, And give your es-tate to a stran-ger.

99   *kept by a Jew* Wealthy Jewish merchants and financiers made a major contribution
       to the development of the City of London as an important financial centre in this
       period but anti-Semitism was rife and emancipation, giving Jews citizenship rights,
       was not achieved in Britain until 1856. In the second illustration in Hogarth's print
       series *A Harlot's Progress* (1732), the harlot is the mistress of a rich Jew.

99   *bating* leaving aside.

104   *bleed freely* spend profligately, in both financial and sexual terms.

104–5 *sent . . . plantations* i.e. by ruining them because of the money they have spent on
       her, causing them to turn to crime and consequent punishment by transportation.

109   *Air 24 When . . . Wife* The title given here to the tune more generally known as 'The
       King's Delight' is from the refrain line of a ballad 'The Benefit of Marriage' (1663–4).
       It was widely disseminated in the period. No specific reference seems intended here.

JENNY DIVER

The gamesters and lawyers are jugglers alike,   110
    If they meddle, your all is in danger.
Like gypsies, if once they can finger a souse,
Your pockets they pick, and they pilfer your house,
    And give your estate to a stranger.

JENNY DIVER

A man of courage should never put anything to the risk but his   115
life. (*She takes up his pistol*) These are the tools of a man of
honour. Cards and dice are fit only for cowardly cheats, who
prey upon their friends.

SUKY TAWDRY

(TAWDRY *takes up the other* [*pistol*]) This, sir, is fitter for your
hand. Besides your loss of money, 'tis a loss to the ladies.   120
Gaming takes you off from women. How fond could I be of you!
But before company 'tis ill bred.

MACHEATH

Wanton hussies!

JENNY

I must and will have a kiss to give my wine a zest.

They take him about the neck and make signs to
PEACHUM *and* CONSTABLES, *who rush in upon him.*

[ACT II,] SCENE v

To them [*enter*] PEACHUM *and* CONSTABLES

PEACHUM

I seize you, sir, as my prisoner.

MACHEATH

Was this well done, Jenny? – Women are decoy ducks; who can
trust them? Beasts, jades, jilts, harpies, Furies, whores!

---

112   *souse* or sou, a coin worth very little.
115–6   *A man . . . life* O2; not in O1.
116   s.d. *She . . . pistol* ed. Continuous with s.d. at 119 in originals.
124   *I . . . kiss* The gesture recalls the betrayal of Christ by Judas.

2   *Was . . . done?* An echo of *Antony and Cleopatra* V.ii.325, 'Is this well done?' which
    is addressed by a guard to Charmian on discovering the body of Cleopatra.

PEACHUM

Your case, Mr Macheath, is not particular. The greatest heroes
have been ruined by women. But, to do them justice, I must own   5
they are a pretty sort of creatures, if we could trust them. You
must now, sir, take your leave of the ladies, and if they have a
mind to make you a visit, they will be sure to find you at home.
This gentleman, ladies, lodges in Newgate. Constables, wait
upon the Captain to his lodgings.   10

Air 25   When I First Laid Siege to my Chloris   [Anon]

MACHEATH

At the tree I shall suffer with pleasure,
At the tree I shall suffer with pleasure;
Let me go where I will,
In all kinds of ill,
I shall find no such furies as these are.   15

PEACHUM

Ladies, I'll take care the reckoning shall be discharged.

(*Exit* MACHEATH, *guarded with* PEACHUM *and* CONSTABLES)

---

3   *jades . . . harpies . . . Furies* A jade is a worn-out horse, applied by extension as a
      term of abuse for a woman. In classical mythology, harpies are rapacious monsters
      with a woman's face and body and the wings and claws of a bird; the Furies are the
      three goddesses of revenge and punishment, represented with snakes entwined in
      their hair.

4   *particular* unique.

10   *Air 25 When . . . Chloris* The first line of a song in Sedley's comedy *Bellamira*
      (1687). There is no connection between these lyrics and Gay's.

16   *reckoning . . . discharged* the bill (for drink) will be paid.

[ACT II,] SCENE vi

The women remain

MRS VIXEN

Look ye, Mrs Jenny, though Mr Peachum may have made a private bargain with you and Suky Tawdry for betraying the Captain, as we were all assisting, we ought all to share alike.

MRS COAXER

I think Mr Peachum, after so long an acquaintance, might have trusted me as well as Jenny Diver.   5

MRS SLAMMEKIN

I am sure at least three men of his hanging, and in a year's time too, if he did me justice, should be set down to my account.

DOLLY TRULL

Mrs Slammekin, that is not fair. For you know one of them was taken in bed with me.

JENNY DIVER

As far as a bowl of punch or a treat, I believe Mrs Suky will join   10
with me. As for anything else, ladies, you cannot in conscience expect it.

MRS SLAMMEKIN

Dear madam –

DOLLY TRULL

I would not for the world –

MRS SLAMMEKIN

'Tis impossible for me –   15

DOLLY TRULL

As I hope to be saved, madam –

MRS SLAMMEKIN

Nay then, I must stay here all night –

DOLLY TRULL

Since you command me.

Exeunt [all the women] with great ceremony

6   *in . . . time* in the space of the past year.
10 *treat* free food or drink.
13–18 and s.d. *Dear madam . . . ceremony* As the stage direction suggests, the prostitutes' leave-taking burlesques the behaviour of polite society.

[ACT II,] SCENE vii

[Scene,] Newgate

[Enter] LOCKIT, TURNKEYS, MACHEATH, CONSTABLES

LOCKIT

Noble Captain, you are welcome. You have not been a lodger of mine this year and a half. You know the custom, sir. Garnish, Captain, garnish. [*To* TURNKEYS] Hand me down those fetters there.

MACHEATH

Those, Mr Lockit, seem to be the heaviest of the whole set. With 5 your leave, I should like the further pair better.

LOCKIT

Look ye, Captain, we know what is fittest for our prisoners. When a gentlemen uses me with civility, I always do the best I can to please him. Hand them down I say. We have them of all prices, from one guinea to ten, and 'tis fitting every gentleman 10 should please himself.

MACHEATH

I understand you, sir. (*Gives money*) The fees here are so many, and so exorbitant, that few fortunes can bear the expense of getting off handsomely, or of dying like a gentleman.

LOCKIT

Those, I see, will fit the Captain better. Take down the further 15 pair. Do but examine them, sir. Never was better work. How genteelly they are made! They will sit as easy as a glove, and the nicest man in England might not be ashamed to wear them. (*He puts on the chains*) If I had the best gentleman in the land in my

---

2 *Garnish* 'Money extorted from a new prisoner, either as a jailer's fee, or as drink-money for the other prisoners' (*OED*), a term first recorded in the sixteenth century; the system of extracting such payment was not abolished until the early nineteenth. Prisons were run as private commercial enterprises and were often corrupt.

3 *fetters* Technically, fetters are leg-irons, and fixed to the wall. Hogarth's picture, however, depicts Macheath with handcuffs, and with leg-irons in an inverted 'V' shape, fixed, presumably, to a belt.

9–10 *We have . . . all prices* Macheath's careful choice of fetters is an obvious burlesque of the man of fashion out shopping (see Introduction, p. xviii).

18 *nicest* most particular.

custody, I could not equip him more handsomely. And so, sir, I   20
now leave you to your private meditations.

                [*Exeunt* LOCKIT, TURNKEYS, CONSTABLES]

[ACT II,] SCENE viii

MACHEATH [*remains, alone*]

Air 26   Courtiers, Courtiers, Think it no Harm   [Anon]

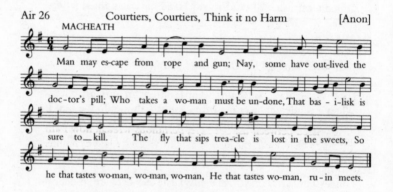

MACHEATH

Man may escape from rope and gun;
Nay, some have outlived the doctor's pill;
Who takes a woman must be undone,
    That basilisk is sure to kill.
The fly that sips treacle is lost in the sweets,   5
So he that tastes woman, woman, woman,
    He that tastes woman, ruin meets.

MACHEATH

To what a woeful plight have I brought myself! Here must I, all
day long till I am hanged, be confined to hear the reproaches of

0   *Air 26 Courtiers . . . Harm* The tune may have originated in the theatre, as a later
     addition to Brome's comedy, *A Jovial Crew*. Its idealising lyric contrasts the
     innocent contentment of a rural couple with the life of the courtier.
1   *may escape* The music in Q1 gives a crotchet for the second note implying an
     elision 'may'escape'; to turn this into two quavers is easier to sing.
4   *basilisk* mythical reptile whose breath and look were fatal.

a wench who lays her ruin at my door. I am in the custody of her 10
father, and to be sure, if he knows of the matter, I shall have a
fine time on't betwixt this and my execution. But I promised the
wench marriage. – What signifies a promise to a woman? Does
not man in marriage itself promise a hundred things that he
never means to perform? Do all we can, women will believe us, 15
for they look upon a promise as an excuse for following their
own inclinations. – But here comes Lucy, and I cannot get from
her. – Would I were deaf!

[ACT II,] SCENE ix

MACHEATH [*remains; enter to him*] LUCY

LUCY

You base man you! How can you look me in the face after what
hath passed between us? See here, perfidious wretch, how I am
forced to bear about the load of infamy you have laid upon me.
Oh, Macheath, thou hast robbed me of my quiet – to see thee
tortured would give me pleasure. 5

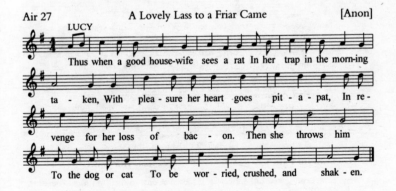

Air 27   A Lovely Lass to a Friar Came   [Anon]

LUCY
Thus when a good house-wife sees a rat In her trap in the morn-ing
ta-ken, With plea-sure her heart goes pit-a-pat, In revenge for her loss of bac-on. Then she throws him
To the dog or cat To be wor-ried, crushed, and shak-en.

---

3   *load of infamy* i.e. her visible pregnancy.
5   *Air 27 A Lovely . . . Came* A tune first recorded in 1710, but probably older. It sets a narrative of a girl confessing sexual transgression to a friar.

LUCY

Thus when a good housewife sees a rat
   In her trap in the morning taken,
With pleasure her heart goes pit-a-pat,
   In revenge for her loss of bacon.
      Then she throws him 10
      To the dog or cat
To be worried, crushed, and shaken.

MACHEATH

Have you no bowels, no tenderness, my dear Lucy, to see a
husband in these circumstances?

LUCY

A husband! 15

MACHEATH

In every respect but the form, and that, my dear, may be said
over us at any time. Friends should not insist upon ceremonies.
From a man of honour, his word is as good as his bond.

LUCY

'Tis the pleasure of all you fine men to insult the women you
have ruined. 20

Air 28   'Twas when the Sea was Roaring   [Handel]

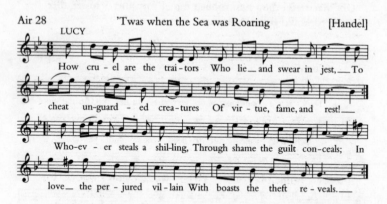

How cru-el are the trai-tors Who lie and swear in jest, To
cheat un-guard-ed crea-tures Of vir-tue, fame, and rest!
Who-ev-er steals a shil-ling, Through shame the guilt con-ceals; In
love the per-jured vil-lain With boasts the theft re-veals.

---

13   *bowels* considered to be the seat of the emotions, so used to mean sympathetic
     feeling or pity.

20   *Air 28 'Twas ... Roaring* The song originated in Gay's tragicomic farce, *The What
     D'ye Call It* (1715), where it is a ballad sung by a woman bewailing the loss of her
     lover at sea, set to a tune probably composed for it by Handel. It prompted several
     political parodies, including one entitled 'The Pretender's Flight', before Gay
     himself took it up again here.

LUCY

How cruel are the traitors
　　Who lie and swear in jest,
To cheat unguarded creatures
　　Of virtue, fame, and rest!
Whoever steals a shilling,   25
　　Through shame the guilt conceals;
In love the perjured villain
　　With boasts the theft reveals.

MACHEATH

The very first opportunity, my dear (have but patience) you
shall be my wife in whatever manner you please.   30

LUCY

Insinuating monster! And so you think I know nothing of the
affair of Miss Polly Peachum? I could tear thy eyes out!

MACHEATH

Sure, Lucy, you can't be such a fool as to be jealous of Polly!

LUCY

Are you not married to her, you brute, you?

MACHEATH

Married! Very good. The wench gives it out only to vex thee, and   35
to ruin me in thy good opinion. 'Tis true, I go to the house; I
chat with the girl, I kiss her, I say a thousand things to her, as all
gentlemen do, that mean nothing, to divert myself; and now the
silly jade hath set it about that I am married to her, to let me know
what she would be at. Indeed, my dear Lucy, these violent passions   40
may be of ill consequence to a woman in your condition.

LUCY

Come, come, Captain, for all your assurance, you know that
Miss Polly hath put it out of your power to do me the justice you
promised me.

MACHEATH

A jealous woman believes everything her passion suggests. To   45
convince you of my sincerity, if we can find the Ordinary, I shall
have no scruples of making you my wife; and I know the
consequences of having two at a time.

31　*Insinuating* Wheedling, ingratiating.　sycophantic
46　*find the Ordinary* i.e. to marry them. See note to I.vi.28–9.
48　*consequences . . . time* Bigamy is a felony and, until the late seventeenth century, was
　　punishable by death. At this period, the punishment was transportation for seven
　　years or imprisonment for two with or without hard labour.

LUCY

That you are only to be hanged, and so get rid of them both.

MACHEATH

I am ready, my dear Lucy, to give you satisfaction – if you think   50
there is any in marriage. What can a man of honour say more?

LUCY

So then, it seems, you are not married to Miss Polly.

MACHEATH

You know, Lucy, the girl is prodigiously conceited. No man can
say a civil thing to her but, like other fine ladies, her vanity
makes her think he's her own for ever and ever.   55

Air 29   The Sun had Loosed his Weary Teams   [Anon]

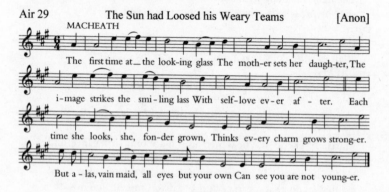

MACHEATH

The first time at the looking glass
    The mother sets her daughter,
The image strikes the smiling lass
    With self-love ever after.
Each time she looks, she, fonder grown,   60
    Thinks every charm grows stronger.
But alas, vain maid, all eyes but your own
    Can see you are not younger.

MACHEATH

When women consider their own beauties, they are all alike
unreasonable in their demands; for they expect their lovers   65
should like them as long as they like themselves.

55   *Air 29 The Sun . . . Teams* originally known as 'The Hemp-Dresser, or the London
     Gentlewoman', the tune acquired the title given here when it was set to a ballad
     beginning with these words by D'Urfey.

LUCY

Yonder is my father – perhaps this way we may light upon the Ordinary, who shall try if you will be as good as your word; for I long to be made an honest woman.

[*Exeunt* MACHEATH *and* LUCY]

[ACT II,] SCENE x

[*Enter*] PEACHUM [*and*] LOCKIT *with an account book*

LOCKIT

In this last affair, brother Peachum, we are agreed. You have consented to go halves in Macheath.

PEACHUM

We shall never fall out about an execution. But as to that article, pray how stands our last year's account?

LOCKIT

If you will run your eye over it, you'll find 'tis fair and clearly   5
stated.

PEACHUM

This long arrear of the government is very hard upon us! Can it be expected that we should hang our acquaintance for nothing, when our betters will hardly save theirs without being paid for it? Unless the people in employment pay better, I promise them   10
for the future, I shall let other rogues live besides their own.

LOCKIT

Perhaps, brother, they are afraid these matters may be carried too far. We are treated by them with contempt, as if our profession were not reputable.

---

69 s.d. ed. There is no stage direction in the originals. The stage must be cleared for the next scene, but that Lucy sees her father approaching seems to indicate that there was no change of scenery.

II, x A letter from Swift to Gay (28 March 1728) suggests that this scene was modelled on the quarrel between Brutus and Cassius in Shakespeare's *Julius Caesar*, IV.iii.

7 *long arrear of the government* delay in the government paying the £40 reward for evidence which led to the conviction and execution of criminals.

10 *people in employment* i.e. the employers, the government.

PEACHUM

In one respect, indeed, our employment may be reckoned   15
dishonest, because, like great statesmen, we encourage those
who betray their friends.

LOCKIT

Such language, brother, anywhere else, might turn to your
prejudice. Learn to be more guarded, I beg you.

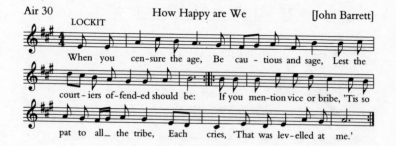

Air 30   How Happy are We   [John Barrett]

LOCKIT

When you cen-sure the age, Be cau-tious and sage, Lest the
court-iers of-fend-ed should be: If you men-tion vice or bribe, 'Tis so
pat to all_ the tribe, Each cries, 'That was lev-elled at me.'

LOCKIT

   When you censure the age,   20
   Be cautious and sage,
Lest the courtiers offended should be:
   If you mention vice or bribe,
   'Tis so pat to all the tribe,
Each cries, 'That was levelled at me.'   25

PEACHUM

Here's poor Ned Clincher's name, I see. Sure, brother Lockit,
there was a little unfair proceeding in Ned's case, for he told me

16 *like great statesmen* This explicit comparison, together with the way in which
Peachum and Lockit address each other as 'brother', reinforces contemporary
audiences' reading of this scene as a satire on the increasingly uneasy relationship
between Walpole and his brother-in-law and former political ally, Charles
Townshend, secretary of state for foreign affairs.

19 *Air 30 How ... We* the first line of a song in Thomas Baker, *The Fine Lady's Airs*
(1708) published on a song-sheet as 'A New Song ... sung by Mr Pack in the figure
of a bawd composd by Mr Barret' (1709).

24 *pat ... tribe* exactly suitable or fitting to all courtiers.

26 *Clincher's name* Clincher is literally a punster, or one who makes smart repartee.
There might be an allusion to Swift's poem 'Clever Tom Clinch going to be hanged'
of 1726 or 1727, which, like *The Beggar's Opera*, refers to Jonathan Wild (see
Introduction, pp. xiv–xv).

in the condemned hold that for value received you had promised
him a session or two longer without molestation.

LOCKIT

Mr Peachum, this is the first time my honour was ever called in   30
question.

PEACHUM

Business is at an end if once we act dishonourably.

LOCKIT

Who accuses me?

PEACHUM

You are warm, brother.

LOCKIT

He that attacks my honour attacks my livelihood, and this usage   35
– sir – is not to be borne.

PEACHUM

Since you provoke me to speak, I must tell you too, that Mrs
Coaxer charges you with defrauding her of her information
money for the apprehending of curl-pated Hugh. Indeed,
indeed, brother, we must punctually pay our spies, or we shall   40
have no information.

LOCKIT

Is this language to me, sirrah, who have saved you from the
gallows, sirrah!

Collaring each other

PEACHUM

If I am hanged, it shall be for ridding the world of an arrant
rascal.   45

LOCKIT

This hand shall do the office of the halter you deserve, and
throttle you, you dog!

PEACHUM

Brother, brother – we are both in the wrong. We shall be both
losers in the dispute, for you know we have it in our power to
hang each other. You should not be so passionate.   50

LOCKIT

Nor you so provoking.

28   *hold* cell.
34   *warm* hot-tempered, angry.
44   s.d. *Collaring each other* grabbing each other by the neck. The scene was once
      thought to parody a quarrel in which Walpole and Townshend 'collared' each other,
      but the play predates that event, presaging rather than reflecting actuality.
46   *halter* noose.

PEACHUM

'Tis our mutual interest; 'tis for the interest of the world we should agree. If I said any thing, brother, to the prejudice of your character, I ask pardon.

LOCKIT

Brother Peachum, I can forgive as well as resent. Give me your   55
hand. Suspicion does not become a friend.

PEACHUM

I only meant to give you occasion to justify yourself. But I must now step home, for I expect the gentleman about this snuff-box that Filch nimmed two nights ago in the park. I appointed him at this hour.   [*Exit*]   60

[ACT II,] SCENE xi

LOCKIT [*remains; to him enter*] LUCY

LOCKIT

Whence come you, hussy?

LUCY

My tears might answer that question.

LOCKIT

You have then been whimpering and fondling like a spaniel over that fellow that hath abused you.

LUCY

One can't help love; one can't cure it. 'Tis not in my power to   5
obey you, and hate him.

LOCKIT

Learn to bear your husband's death like a reasonable woman. 'Tis not the fashion, nowadays, so much as to affect sorrow upon these occasions. No woman would ever marry, if she had not the chance of mortality for a release. Act like a woman of   10
spirit, hussy, and thank your father for what he is doing.

59   *nimmed* stole.

      the park most likely to be St James's Park, just south of the then official royal residence of St James's Palace. Popular with people of fashion as a place to walk and therefore also a hunting ground for thieves and prostitutes.

8   *affect* give the appearance of, pretend to.

Air 31   Of Noble Race was Shenkin   [Thomas D'Urfey]

Is then his fate decreed, sir? Such a man can I think of quitting? When first we met, so moves me yet, Oh, see how my heart is splitting.

LUCY

Is then his fate decreed, sir?
    Such a man can I think of quitting?
When first we met, so moves me yet,
    Oh, see how my heart is splitting!   15

LOCKIT

Look ye, Lucy, there is no saving him. So, I think, you must even do like other widows – buy yourself weeds, and be cheerful.

Air 32   [Untitled]   [Anon]

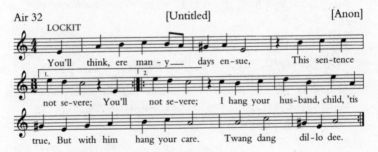

You'll think, ere man-y days en-sue, This sen-tence not se-vere; You'll not se-vere; I hang your hus-band, child, 'tis true, But with him hang your care. Twang dang dil-lo dee.

LOCKIT

You'll think, ere many days ensue,
    This sentence not severe;

11   *Air 31 Of . . . Shenkin* The tune takes its name from a song in D'Urfey's *The Richmond Heiress* (1693). It was sung to a Welsh harp which played the notes here given to the violin. It was set to a number of songs, including a Jacobite ballad, 'Of doubtful race was Georgy'.

17   *weeds* mourning clothes.
      Air 32 The untitled air has affinities with the tune 'Walsingham', most closely associated in theatrical tradition with Ophelia's song 'How should I your true love know' in *Hamlet*. Lockit's cynical advice jars with the melancholy of the air. The '*b*' in bar three is from Q1, '*e*' in O1 and O2.

67

> I hang your husband, child, 'tis true, 20
>> But with him hang your care.
>> Twang dang dillo dee.

LOCKIT

Like a good wife, go moan over your dying husband. That, child, is your duty. Consider, girl, you can't have the man and the money too. So make yourself as easy as you can, by getting all 25 you can from him. [*Exit*]

[ACT II,] SCENE xii

LUCY [*remains, to her enter*] MACHEATH

LUCY

Though the Ordinary was out of the way today, I hope, my dear, you will upon the first opportunity quiet my scruples. Oh sir! My father's hard heart is not to be softened, and I am in the utmost despair.

MACHEATH

But if I could raise a small sum – would not twenty guineas, 5 think you, move him? Of all the arguments in the way of business, the perquisite is the most prevailing. Your father's perquisites for the escape of prisoners must amount to a considerable sum in the year. Money well timed and properly applied will do anything. 10

Air 33   London Ladies   [Thomas D'Urfey]

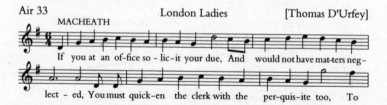

MACHEATH

If you at an of-fice so - lic-it your due, And would not have mat-ters neg-lect - ed, You must quick-en the clerk with the per-quis-ite too, To

---

0   s.d. Editors have suggested that the scene changes here to Macheath's cell, where he is discovered and Lucy comes to him. This change, though possible, is not necessary, since all the action could remain in the generalised space of Newgate from II.vii through to this scene.

7   *perquisite* usually meaning a tip, but used here as a euphemism for a bribe.

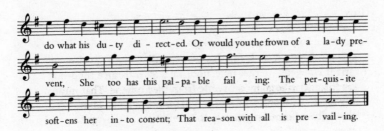

do what his du-ty di-rect-ed. Or would you the frown of a la-dy pre-

vent, She too has this pal-pa-ble fail-ing: The per-quis-ite

soft-ens her in-to consent; That rea-son with all is pre-vail-ing.

MACHEATH

If you at an office solicit your due,
    And would not have matters neglected,
You must quicken the clerk with the perquisite too,
    To do what his duty directed.
Or would you the frowns of a lady prevent,   15
    She too has this palpable failing:
The perquisite softens her into consent;
    That reason with all is prevailing.

LUCY

What love or money can do shall be done; for all my comfort
depends upon your safety.   20

[ACT II,] SCENE xiii

LUCY, MACHEATH [*remain; to them enter*] POLLY

POLLY

Where is my dear husband? Was a rope ever intended for this
neck? O let me throw my arms about it, and throttle thee with
love! – Why dost thou turn away from me? – 'Tis thy Polly – 'tis
thy wife!

MACHEATH

[*Aside*] Was there ever such an unfortunate rascal as I am?   5

10 *Air 33 London Ladies* D'Urfey's song 'Ladies of London, both wealthy and fair' first
    appeared in 1687, set to this tune. It spawned a number of answering 'advice'
    poems, and Macheath's lyric continues in this vein.

13 *quicken* rouse, motivate; in other words, bribe into the action which helps the
    prisoner.

LUCY

[*Aside*] Was there ever such another villain?

POLLY

Oh Macheath! Was it for this we parted? Taken! Imprisoned!
Tried! Hanged! – Cruel reflection! I'll stay with thee till death;
no force shall tear thy dear wife from thee now. – What means
my love? – Not one kind word? Not one kind look? Think what   10
thy Polly suffers to see thee in this condition.

Air 34   All in the Downs   [Pietro G. Sandoni]

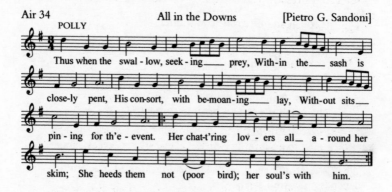

POLLY

Thus when the swallow, seeking prey,
   Within the sash is closely pent,
His consort, with bemoaning lay,
   Without sits pining for th' event.   15
Her chatt'ring lovers all around her skim;
She heeds them not (poor bird); her soul's with him.

10   *word? . . . look?* These are exclamation marks in the original, which might suggest a
     different mode of address, in which Polly exclaims aside to the audience, rather than
     Macheath.

11   *Air 34 All . . . Downs* The title is the first line of Gay's poem 'Sweet William's Farewell
     to black-ey'd Susan', which tells of their mutual sorrow as William's boat sets sail,
     sentiments that are commensurate with Polly's in this song. The poem was set by a
     number of composers.

13   *Within . . . pent* Imprisoned behind a sash window. The image is of a swallow which
     has strayed into a house.

14   *consort* partner. Swallows mate for life.   *lay* song.

15   *Without* Outside.

     for th' event ambiguous; could mean either 'because of what has happened' or 'in
     anticipation of the inevitable outcome'.

MACHEATH

(*Aside*) I must disown her. [*To* LUCY] The wench is distracted.

LUCY

Am I then bilked of my virtue? Can I have no reparation? Sure
men were born to lie, and women to believe them! O villain,   20
villain!

POLLY

Am I not thy wife? Thy neglect of me, thy aversion to me, too
severely proves it. – Look on me. – Tell me, am I not thy wife?

LUCY

Perfidious wretch!

POLLY

Barbarous husband!   25

LUCY

Hadst thou been hanged five months ago, I had been happy.

POLLY

And I too. If you had been kind to me till death, it would not
have vexed me. And that's no very unreasonable request (though
from a wife) to a man who hath not above seven or eight days to
live.   30

LUCY

Art thou then married to another? Hast thou two wives,
monster?

MACHEATH

If women's tongues can cease for an answer, hear me.

LUCY

I won't. Flesh and blood can't bear my usage.

POLLY

Shall I not claim my own? Justice bids me speak.   35

Air 35   Have you Heard of a Frolicsome Ditty   [Anon]

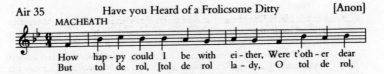

18   s.d. *Aside* Placed between the two phrases in original texts, but must apply only to
     the first.
19   *bilked* cheated.
34   *my usage* the way I've been treated.
35   *Air 35 Have . . . Ditty* The tune, known by different names, dates from the mid
     seventeenth century, and has a complex history. This title derives from a ballad
     entitled 'The Jolly Gentleman's frolick: or the City Ramble'.

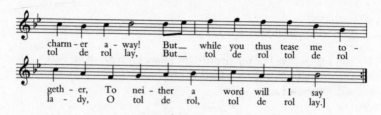

MACHEATH

How happy could I be with either,
Were t'other dear charmer away!
But while you thus tease me together,
To neither a word will I say
But tol de rol, etc.   40

POLLY

Sure, my dear, there ought to be some preference shown to a
wife! At least she may claim the appearance of it. [*Aside*] He
must be distracted with his misfortunes, or he could not use me
thus.

LUCY

O villain, villain! Thou hast deceived me. I could even inform   45
against thee with pleasure. Not a prude wishes more heartily to
have facts against her intimate acquaintance than I now wish to
have facts against thee. I would have her satisfaction, and they
should all out.

Air 36   Irish Trot   [Anon]

POLLY   LUCY   POLLY   LUCY
I'm bub-bled. I'm bub-bled. Oh how I am troub-led! Bam - booz-led, and

POLLY   [Fine] LUCY
bit! My dis - tres-es are doub-led. When you come to the tree, should the

[D.C. al Fine]
hang-man re-fuse, These fing-ers, with plea-sure, could fast-en the noose.

36 *How . . . either* This song is commonly read as a satirical comment on Walpole. See
    note to I.iv.5.
48 *facts* evidence. 'Fact' at this period still retained some of its meaning, common in
    the sixteenth and seventeenth centuries, of 'an evil deed, a crime'.

POLLY

I'm bubbled.

LUCY

I'm bubbled.   50

POLLY

O how I am troubled!

LUCY

Bamboozled, and bit!

POLLY

My distresses are doubled.

LUCY

When you come to the tree, should the hangman refuse,
These fingers, with pleasure, could fasten the noose.

POLLY

I'm bubbled, etc.   55

MACHEATH

[*To* LUCY] Be pacified, my dear Lucy – this is all a fetch of Polly's
to make me desperate with you in case I get off. If I am hanged,
she would fain have the credit of being thought my widow. [*To*
POLLY] Really, Polly, this is no time for a dispute of this sort; for
whenever you are talking of marriage, I am thinking of hanging.   60

POLLY

And hast thou the heart to persist in disowning me?

MACHEATH

And hast thou the heart to persist in persuading me that I am
married? Why, Polly, dost thou seek to aggravate my
misfortunes?

LUCY

Really, Miss Peachum, you but expose yourself. Besides, 'tis   65
barbarous in you to worry a gentleman in his circumstances.

---

49   *Air 36 Irish Trot* The tune for a ribald ballad, 'One night in my ramble'. The musical
      text has no repeats, but the printed lyric implies one, either, as here, of the first part
      of the tune, or of all of it.
50–5 *I'm bubbled . . . I'm bubbled* The sharing of the vocal lines between Polly and Lucy
      here reflects their shared situation, and burlesques the duets sung in similar
      situations of conflicted love in contemporary Italian opera.
50   *bubbled* fooled, cheated.
52   *bit* tricked.
56   *fetch* trick.
57   *make . . . you* to make you furious with me.

Air 37   [Untitled]   [Anon]

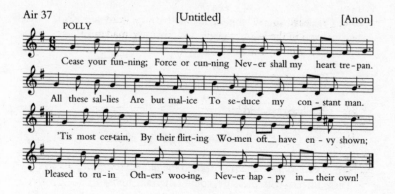

POLLY

Cease your fun-ning; Force or cun-ning Nev-er shall my heart tre-pan.

All these sal-lies Are but mal-ice To se-duce my con - stant man.

'Tis most cer-tain, By their flirt-ing Wo-men oft— have en - vy shown;

Pleased to ru-in Oth-ers' woo-ing, Nev-er hap - py in— their own!

POLLY

Cease your funning;
Force or cunning
Never shall my heart trepan.
All these sallies   70
Are but malice
To seduce my constant man.
'Tis most certain,
By their flirting
Women oft have envy shown;   75
Pleased to ruin
Others' wooing,
Never happy in their own!

POLLY

Decency, madam, methinks might teach you to behave yourself
with some reserve with the husband while his wife is present.   80

MACHEATH

But seriously, Polly, this is carrying the joke a little too far.

LUCY

If you are determined, madam, to raise a disturbance in the
prison, I shall be obliged to send for the turnkey to show you the
door. I am sorry, madam, you force me to be so ill-bred.

---

66   *Air 37* This untitled air seems to derive from a tune known as 'Charming Billy' or
'Constant Billy'.
67   *funning* fooling.
69   *trepan* ensnare, beguile (*OED trepan* v[2]).

POLLY

Give me leave to tell you, madam, these forward airs don't 85
become you in the least, madam. And my duty, madam, obliges
me to stay with my husband, madam.

Air 38　　　　　　Good Morrow, Gossip Joan　　　　　[Anon]

LUCY　Why how now, Mad-am　Flirt? If___ you thus must chat-ter,　And
POLLY　Why how now, sau-cy　jade? Sure___ the wench is　tip-sy!　How

are for fling-ing　dirt,　　　　　　　　　　　　　　　　　Let's
can you see me　made　　　　　　　　　　　　　　　　　The

try　who best can　spat - - - ter,　Ma - dam　Flirt!
scoff　of such　a　gyp - - - sy?　Sau - cy　jade!

LUCY

Why how now, Madam Flirt?
If you thus must chatter,
And are for flinging dirt, 90
Let's try who best can spatter,
Madam Flirt!

POLLY

Why how now, saucy jade?
Sure the wench is tipsy!
(*To him*) How can you see me made 95
The scoff of such a gipsy?
(*To her*) Saucy jade!

87　*Air 38 Good . . . Joan* The tune is a variant on 'Good morrow, Gossip Joan' (1705),
a ballad whose words have no resonance for Gay's song. Key signature three sharps
in Q1. In the music the extended runs on single syllables – 'dirt' and 'made' – are
unusual in the word-setting of this opera, and the vocal elaboration suggests that
Gay is satirising the infamous quarrel between the Italian sopranos Faustina and
Cuzzoni.

[ACT II,] SCENE xiv

LUCY, MACHEATH, POLLY [*remain; to them enter*] PEACHUM

PEACHUM

Where's my wench? Ah, hussy, hussy! Come you home, you slut;
and when your fellow is hanged, hang yourself, to make your
family some amends.

POLLY

Dear, dear father, do not tear me from him – I must speak; I have
more to say to him. – [*To* MACHEATH] Oh! Twist thy fetters
about me, that he may not haul me from thee!

PEACHUM

Sure all women are alike! If ever they commit the folly, they are
sure to commit another by exposing themselves. Away! Not a
word more! You are my prisoner now, hussy.

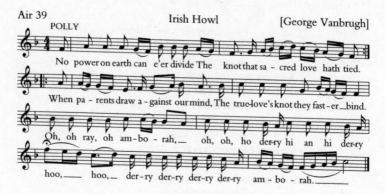

Air 39   Irish Howl   [George Vanbrugh]

POLLY
No power on earth can e'er divide The knot that sa - cred love hath tied.

When pa - rents draw a - gainst our mind, The true-love's knot they fast-er bind.

Oh, oh ray, oh am-bo - rah,— oh, oh, ho der-ry hi an hi der-ry

hoo,— hoo,— der-ry der-ry der-ry der-ry am - bo - rah.

POLLY

No power on earth can e'er divide
The knot that sacred love hath tied.

7   *commit the folly* engage in a sexual relationship; 'folly', meaning 'lewdness,
wantonness' was becoming obsolete at this period (see *OED* 3a and 3b) but is
clearly still active here.

9   *Air 39 Irish Howl* From the title 'Celias Complaint or the Irish Howle by Mr
Vanbrughe', a lyric of female complaint at desertion, which potentially might
undercut Polly's assertion of the power of love. The 'words' of the first two bars of
the nonsense refrain underlaid to the music in Q1 are slightly different from those
printed in its text.

When parents draw against our mind,
The true-love's knot they faster bind,
   Oh, oh ray, oh Amborah--oh, oh, etc.

[POLLY] *holding* MACHEATH; PEACHUM *pulling her*
      [*drags her offstage*]

[ACT II,] SCENE xv

LUCY [*and*] MACHEATH [*remain*]   5

MACHEATH

I am naturally compassionate, wife; so I could not use the wench as she deserved; which made you at first suspect there was something in what she said.

LUCY

Indeed, my dear, I was strangely puzzled.   10

MACHEATH

If that had been the case, her father would never have brought me into this circumstance. No, Lucy, I had rather die than be false to thee.

LUCY

How happy am I, if you say this from your heart! For I love thee so, that I could sooner bear to see thee hanged than in the arms of another.

MACHEATH

But could'st thou bear to see me hanged?

LUCY

Oh Macheath, I can never live to see that day.

MACHEATH

You see, Lucy, in the account of love you are in my debt, and you must now be convinced that I rather choose to die than be another's. Make me, if possible, love thee more, and let me owe my life to thee. If you refuse to assist me, Peachum and your father will immediately put me beyond all means of escape.

LUCY

My father, I know, hath been drinking hard with the prisoners; and I fancy he is now taking his nap in his own room. If I can procure the keys, shall I go off with thee, my dear?   5

MACHEATH

If we are together 'twill be impossible to lie concealed. As soon as the search begins to be a little cool, I will send to thee. Till then my heart is thy prisoner.

LUCY   10

Come then, my dear husband, owe thy life to me; and though you love me not, be grateful – but that Polly runs in my head strangely.

MACHEATH

A moment of time may make us unhappy for ever.

Air 40   The Lass of Patie's Mill   [Anon]

I like the fox shall grieve,—Whose mate hath left her side, Whom hounds from morn to eve— Chase o'er— the coun - try wide. Where can my lov-er hide? Where cheat— the wea - ry— pack? If love be not his guide,— He nev - er— will come back!

LUCY

I like the fox shall grieve,
    Whose mate hath left her side,
Whom hounds from morn to eve   15
    Chase o'er the country wide.
Where can my lover hide?
    Where cheat the weary pack?
If love be not his guide,
    He never will come back!

[*Exeunt*]   20

---

26   *Air 40 The Lass . . . Mill* The first line and title of a straightforwardly celebratory love-song of a male speaker by Allan Ramsay, published in 1724. The tune is much older, dating back at least to the mid-seventeenth century. The versions of the tune in O1 and O2 differ in details from that in Q1.

32   *weary* As O1 and early states of O2. Later states of O2 and Q1 print 'wary', which is a possible reading, adopted by some editors.

Scene, Newgate

[*Enter*] LOCKIT [*and*] LUCY

LOCKIT

To be sure, wench, you must have been aiding and abetting to help him to this escape.

LUCY

Sir, here hath been Peachum and his daughter Polly, and to be sure they know the ways of Newgate as well as if they had been born and bred in the place all their lives. Why must all your   5 suspicion light upon me?

LOCKIT

Lucy, Lucy, I will have none of these shuffling answers.

LUCY

Well then – if I know anything of him, I wish I may be burnt!

LOCKIT

Keep your temper, Lucy, or I shall pronounce you guilty.

LUCY

Keep yours, sir, – I do wish I may be burnt. I do – and what can   10 I say more to convince you?

LOCKIT

Did he tip handsomely? How much did he come down with? Come, hussy, don't cheat your father, and I shall not be angry with you. Perhaps you have made a better bargain with him than I could have done – how much, my good girl?   15

LUCY

You know, sir, I am fond of him, and would have given money to have kept him with me.

LOCKIT

Ah Lucy! Thy education might have put thee more upon thy guard; for a girl in the bar of an ale-house is always besieged.

LUCY

Dear sir, mention not my education – for 'twas to that I owe my   20 ruin.

---

8   *burnt* referring either to the punishment for women found guilty of treason, which until 1790 was burning to death; or to 'burning in the hand', the branding of first offenders granted benefit of clergy (see note to I.vi.28–9).

Air 41   If Love's a Sweet Passion   [Henry Purcell]

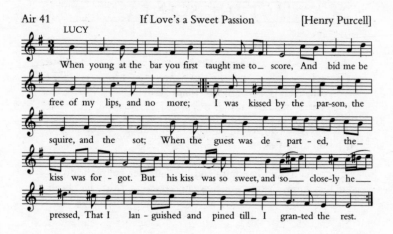

When young at the bar you first taught me to— score, And bid me be free of my lips, and no more; I was kissed by the par-son, the squire, and the sot; When the guest was de-part-ed, the— kiss was for-got. But his kiss was so sweet, and so— close-ly he— pressed, That I lan-guished and pined till— I gran-ted the rest.

LUCY

When young at the bar you first taught me to score,
And bid me be free of my lips, and no more;
I was kissed by the parson, the squire, and the sot;
When the guest was departed, the kiss was forgot.   25
But his kiss was so sweet, and so closely he pressed,
That I languished and pined till I granted the rest.

LUCY

If you can forgive me, sir, I will make a fair confession, for to be sure he hath been a most barbarous villain to me.

LOCKIT

And so you have let him escape, hussy, have you?   30

LUCY

When a woman loves, a kind look, a tender word, can persuade her to anything – and I could ask no other bribe.

LOCKIT

Thou wilt always be a vulgar slut, Lucy. If you would not be

21   *Air 41 If . . . Passion* The title and first line of a song in Purcell's *The Fairy Queen* (1692), which consists of a series of masques inserted into an adaptation of Shakespeare's *A Midsummer Night's Dream.* The song celebrates the combined pain and pleasure of love in conventional terms, and contrasts with Lucy's altogether more down-to-earth experience. The second note in bar 13 is '*b*' in Q1. In O1, O2 the second repeat is only from 'But his kiss'.

22   *score* keep the tally of money owed.

looked upon as a fool, you should never do anything but upon
the foot of interest. Those that act otherwise are their own   35
bubbles.

LUCY

But love, sir, is a misfortune that may happen to the most
discreet woman, and in love we are all fools alike.
Notwithstanding all he swore, I am now fully convinced that
Polly Peachum is actually his wife. Did I let him escape (fool that   40
I was) to go to her? Polly will wheedle herself into his money,
and then Peachum will hang him, and cheat us both.

LOCKIT

And so I am to be ruined, because, forsooth, you must be in
love! A very pretty excuse!

LUCY

I could murder that impudent happy strumpet! I gave him   45
his life, and that creature enjoys the sweets of it. Ungrateful
Macheath!

Air 42   South-Sea Ballad   [Anon]

My love is all madness and folly;— Alone I lie, Toss,
tumble, and cry, What a happy creature is Polly!— Was
e'er such a wretch as I!— With rage I redden like scarlet,—That my
dear inconstant varlet,— Stark blind to my charms, Is lost in the arms Of that
jilt, that inveigling harlot! Stark blind to my charms, Is lost in the arms Of that
jilt, that inveigling harlot! This, this my resentment alarms.—

35–6   *are their own bubbles* make fools of themselves.
47   *Air 42 South-Sea Ballad* There are a number of song-sheet ballads with this title,
      but none with the same tune; the tune is found in *The Dancing Master* (c. 1728)
      entitled 'South Sea'. Any connection with the South-Sea Bubble is probably fortuitous.

LUCY

My love is all madness and folly;
    Alone I lie,
    Toss, tumble, and cry, 50
What a happy creature is Polly!
Was e'er such a wretch as I!
With rage I redden like scarlet,
That my dear inconstant varlet, *→ a dishonest, unprincipled man*
    Stark blind to my charms, 55
    Is lost in the arms
Of that jilt, that inveigling harlot!
    Stark blind to my charms,
    Is lost in the arms
Of that jilt, that inveigling harlot! 60
This, this my resentment alarms.

LOCKIT

And so, after all this mischief, I must stay here to be entertained
with your caterwauling, Mistress Puss! Out of my sight, wanton *howling cat? Tomcat?*
strumpet! You shall fast and mortify yourself into reason, with
now and then a little handsome discipline to bring you to your 65
senses. Go!

[*Exit* LUCY]

[ACT III,] SCENE ii

LOCKIT [*remains, alone*]

LOCKIT

Peachum then intends to outwit me in this affair; but I'll be even
with him. The dog is leaky in his liquor, so I'll ply him that way,
get the secret from him, and turn this affair to my own
advantage. Lions, wolves and vultures don't live together in
herds, droves, or flocks. Of all animals of prey, man is the only 5
sociable one. Every one of us preys upon the other, and yet we
herd together. Peachum is my companion, my friend. –
According to the custom of the world, indeed, he may quote

2   *leaky* prone to talk too freely.

thousands of precedents for cheating me – and shall I not make
use of the privilege of friendship to make him a return?   10

Air 43   Packington's Pound   [Anon]

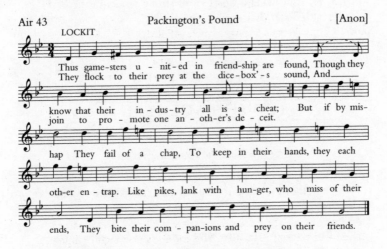

LOCKIT
Thus gamesters united in friendship are found,
Though they know that their industry all is a cheat;
They flock to their prey at the dice-box's sound,
And join to promote one another's deceit.
        But if by mishap   15
        They fail of a chap,
To keep in their hands, they each other entrap.
Like pikes, lank with hunger, who miss of their ends,
They bite their companions and prey on their friends.

LOCKIT
Now, Peachum, you and I, like honest tradesmen, are to have a   20
fair trial which of us can overreach the other. – Lucy!

Enter LUCY

10 *Air 43 Packington's Pound* The tune dates back to the sixteenth century, and was
    enormously popular. It is attached to numerous ballads, none of which seem to
    have specific resonance for Gay's lyric.
16 *fail of a chap* lack a victim (literally, a customer).
18 *pikes* freshwater fish often thought of (not necessarily accurately) as vicious
    predators, partly because they sometimes prey on smaller members of their own
    species.

Are there any of Peachum's people now in the house?

LUCY

Filch, sir, is drinking a quartern of strong waters in the next room with Black Moll.

LOCKIT

Bid him come to me.   25

[*Exit* LUCY]

[ACT III,] SCENE iii

LOCKIT [*remains; to him enter*] FILCH

LOCKIT

Why, boy, thou lookest as if thou wert half starved, like a shotten herring.

FILCH

One had need have the constitution of a horse to go through the business. Since the favourite child-getter was disabled by a mishap, I have picked up a little money by helping the ladies to   5
a pregnancy against their being called down to sentence. But if a man cannot get an honest livelihood any easier way, I am sure, 'tis what I can't undertake for another session.

LOCKIT

Truly, if that great man should tip off, 'twould be an irreparable loss. The vigour and prowess of a knight-errant never saved half   10
the ladies in distress that he hath done. But, boy, canst thou tell me where thy master is to be found?

FILCH

At his lock, sir, at the Crooked Billet.

---

23   *quartern of strong waters* a quarter of a pint of spirits (most likely to be gin).

1–2   *a shotten herring* a herring after spawning, hence implying sexual exhaustion.
4–6   *the favourite . . . sentence* See commentary on I.ii.3. The 'mishap' which has befallen the previous 'child-getter' is probably venereal disease, which is characterised as an 'accident' at III.vi.44.
9   *great man* Referring to the previous 'child-getter'; but from around 1725 Walpole was commonly referred to as 'the great man'. Here the joke is aimed primarily at his sexual appetite.
     tip off die.
13   *lock* Gay footnotes this: 'A cant word, signifying a warehouse where stolen goods are deposited'.

LOCKIT

Very well. I have nothing more with you. (*Exit* FILCH) I'll go to
him there, for I have many important affairs to settle with him;   15
and in the way of these transactions, I'll artfully get into his
secret, so that Macheath shall not remain a day longer out of my
clutches.   [*Exit*]

[ACT III,] SCENE iv

[Scene,] a gaming-house

[Enter] MACHEATH *in a fine tarnished coat,*
BEN BUDGE, MATT OF THE MINT

MACHEATH

I am sorry, gentlemen, the road was so barren of money. When
my friends are in difficulties, I am always glad that my fortune
can be serviceable to them. (*Gives them money*) You see,
gentlemen, I am not a mere court friend, who professes every
thing and will do nothing.   5

Air 44   Lillibulero   [Anon]

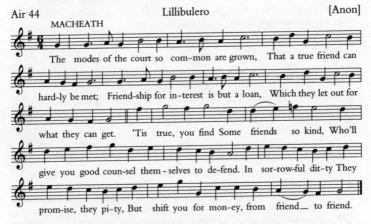

The modes of the court so com-mon are grown, That a true friend can
hard-ly be met; Friend-ship for in-terest is but a loan, Which they let out for
what they can get. 'Tis true, you find Some friends so kind, Who'll
give you good coun-sel them-selves to de-fend. In sor-row-ful dit-ty They
prom-ise, they pi-ty, But shift you for mon-ey, from friend to friend.

s.d.   *fine tarnished coat* an originally expensive coat on which the silver braiding has
      become tarnished.
  5   *Air 44 Lillibulero* The tune, which became popular when associated in 1688 with
      anti-papist lyrics, was certainly older than that. In one source it is attributed to
      Henry Purcell, though he probably arranged, rather than composed the air.

MACHEATH

The modes of the court so common are grown,
   That a true friend can hardly be met;
Friendship for interest is but a loan,
   Which they let out for what they can get.
      'Tis true, you find   10
      Some friends so kind,
Who will give you good counsel themselves to defend.
      In sorrowful ditty
      They promise, they pity,
But shift you for money, from friend to friend.   15

MACHEATH

But we, gentlemen, still have honour enough to break through
the corruptions of the world. And while I can serve you, you
may command me.

BEN BUDGE

It grieves my heart that so generous a man should be involved in
such difficulties as oblige him to live with such ill company, and 20
herd with gamesters.

MATT OF THE MINT

See the partiality of mankind! One man may steal a horse, better
than another may look over a hedge. Of all mechanics, of all
servile handicraftsmen, a gamester is the vilest. But yet, as many
of the quality are of the profession, he is admitted among the 25
politest company. I wonder we are not more respected.

MACHEATH

There will be deep play tonight at Marybone, and consequently
money may be picked up upon the road. Meet me there, and I'll
give you the hint who is worth setting.

MATT OF THE MINT

The fellow with a brown coat with a narrow gold binding, I am 30
told, is never without money.

22–4 *One man . . . hedge* a well-known proverb. The implication is that members of high
society and government can get away with serious crimes whilst those in the lower
and criminal classes are viewed with suspicion even when behaving innocently.

23   *mechanics* manual workers.

27   *deep play* gambling for high stakes.

29   *setting* setting upon, robbing.

30   *fellow . . . binding* The specificity of this description suggests that it might have
referred to some known contemporary figure, though none has been identified.

MACHEATH

What do you mean, Matt? Sure you will not think of meddling with him! He's a good honest kind of a fellow, and one of us.

BEN BUDGE

To be sure, sir, we will put ourselves under your direction.

MACHEATH

Have an eye upon the money-lenders – a rouleau, or two, would   35
prove a pretty sort of an expedition. I hate extortion.

MATT OF THE MINT

Those rouleaus are very pretty things. I hate your bank bills – there is such a hazard in putting them off.

MACHEATH

There is a certain man of distinction, who in his time hath nicked me out of a great deal of the ready. He is in my cash, Ben: 40
I'll point him out to you this evening, and you shall draw upon him for the debt. The company are met; I hear the dice-box in the other room. So, gentlemen, your servant. You'll meet me at Marybone.

[Exeunt]

[ACT III,] SCENE v

[Scene,] PEACHUM*'s lock*
A table with wine, brandy, pipes, and tobacco

[Enter] PEACHUM, LOCKIT

LOCKIT

The Coronation account, brother Peachum, is of so intricate a nature, that I believe it will never be settled.

---

35   *rouleau* gold coins, wrapped in a cylindrical packet, and lent at high rates of interest
to gamblers to be used as stakes at the gambling tables.
37   *bank bills* See note to I.iv.36.
38   *such . . . off* i.e. getting rid of them, cashing them in, is so risky.
40   *nicked me* cheated me; a 'nick' was a winning throw in Hazard, a game played with
dice.
in my cash i.e. has money of mine.

1   *The Coronation account* George II was crowned in October 1727, an opportunity
for thieves to work the large crowds.

PEACHUM

It consists indeed of a great variety of articles. It was worth to
our people, in fees of different kinds, above ten instalments.
This is part of the account, brother, that lies open before us. 5

LOCKIT

[*Reading*] A lady's tail of rich brocade – that, I see, is disposed
of.

PEACHUM

To Mrs Diana Trapes, the tallywoman, and she will make a good
hand on't in shoes and slippers, to trick out young ladies, upon
their going into keeping. 10

LOCKIT

But I don't see any article of the jewels.

PEACHUM

Those are so well known that they must be sent abroad – you'll
find them entered under the article of exportation. As for the
snuff-boxes, watches, swords, etcetera – I thought it best to enter
them under their several heads. 15

LOCKIT

[*Reading*] Seven and twenty women's pockets complete, with
the several things therein contained; all sealed, numbered, and
entered.

PEACHUM

But, brother, it is impossible for us now to enter upon this affair.
We should have the whole day before us. Besides, the account of 20
the last half-year's plate is in a book by itself, which lies at the
other office.

LOCKIT

[*Calls*] Bring us then more liquor! [*To* PEACHUM] Today shall
be for pleasure, tomorrow for business. Ah, brother, those
daughters of ours are two slippery hussies. Keep a watchful eye 25
upon Polly, and Macheath in a day or two shall be our own
again.

6   *tail* the train of a gown. By the 1720s detachable trains were out of fashion other
     than with mantuas (see note to III.vi.13) or for court wear.
8–10 *she . . . keeping* The suggestion is that Mrs Trapes will make shoes out of the
     material of the train as part of her role in providing suitably rich attire for 'kept'
     women, prostitutes who are becoming the mistresses of rich men.
16   *pockets* small bags, not sewn in to garments, but tied round the waist.
21   *plate* tableware made of gold or silver.

Air 45   Down in the North Country   [Anon]

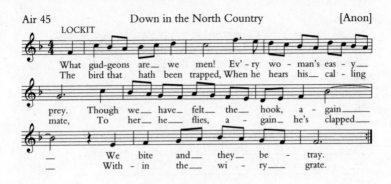

LOCKIT

What gud-geons are— we men! Ev'-ry wo—man's eas-y—
The bird that hath been trapped, When he hears his— cal - ling

prey. Though we have— felt— the— hook, a - gain—
mate, To her— he— flies, a - gain— he's clapped—

—   We bite and— they— be - tray.
—   With - in the— wi - ry— grate.

LOCKIT

What gudgeons are we men!
 Ev'ry woman's easy prey.
Though we have felt the hook, again   30
 We bite and they betray.

The bird that hath been trapped,
 When he hears his calling mate,
To her he flies, again he's clapped
 Within the wiry grate.   35

PEACHUM

But what signifies catching the bird, if your daughter Lucy will
set open the door of the cage?

LOCKIT

If men were answerable for the follies and frailties of their wives
and daughters, no friends could keep a good correspondence
together for two days. This is unkind of you, brother; for among   40
good friends, what they say or do goes for nothing.

Enter a SERVANT

SERVANT

Sir, here's Mrs Diana Trapes wants to speak with you.

PEACHUM

Shall we admit her, brother Lockit?

27   *Air 45 Down . . . Country* The first line of a ballad issued c. 1705 telling of a
     milkmaid who is entranced by a shepherd's bagpipe.
28   *gudgeons* small freshwater fish which are easily caught, so used to mean vulnerable
     fools.
35   *wiry grate* cage.

89

LOCKIT

By all means – she's a good customer, and a fine-spoken woman – and a woman who drinks and talks so freely will enliven the conversation.   45

PEACHUM

Desire her to walk in.

Exit SERVANT

[ACT III,] SCENE vi

PEACHUM [*and*] LOCKIT
[*remain; to them enter*] MRS TRAPES

PEACHUM

Dear Mrs Di, your servant. [*They kiss*] One may know by your kiss that your gin is excellent.

MRS TRAPES

I was always very curious in my liquors.

LOCKIT

There is no perfumed breath like it. I have been long acquainted with the flavour of those lips, han't I, Mrs Di?   5

MRS TRAPES

Fill it up. I take as large draughts of liquor as I did of love. I hate a flincher in either.

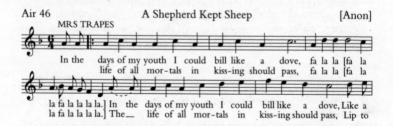

Air 46   A Shepherd Kept Sheep   [Anon]

In the days of my youth I could bill like a dove, fa la la [fa la
life of all mor-tals in kiss-ing should pass, fa la la [fa la

la fa la la la la la.] In the days of my youth I could bill like a dove, Like a
la fa la la la la la.] The__ life of all mor-tals in kiss-ing should pass, Lip to

3   *curious* particular, choosy.
7   *flincher* someone unwilling to join in or, more specifically, 'one who abstains from drinking' (*OED*, 2).
     Air 46 A . . . Sheep The first line of a ballad in *Pills*, 5.35, though the tune is only distantly related to that given here. Barlow suggests that Peachum and Lockit might join in the 'fa la la' refrains.

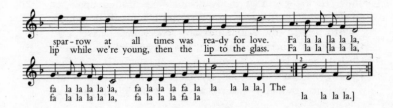

spar - row at all times was rea-dy for love. Fa la la [la la la,
lip while we're young, then the lip to the glass. Fa la la [la la la,

fa la la la la la, fa la la la fa la la la la la.] The
fa la la la la la, fa la la la fa la la la la la.]

MRS TRAPES

In the days of my youth I could bill like a dove, fa, la la, etc.
Like a sparrow, at all times was ready for love. Fa, la la, etc.
The life of all mortals in kissing should pass,   10
Lip to lip while we're young, then the lip to the glass. Fa, la la, etc.

MRS TRAPES

But now, Mr Peachum, to our business. If you have blacks of any
kind brought in of late – mantoes, velvet scarfs, petticoats – let
it be what it will, I am your chap, for all my ladies are very fond
of mourning.   15

PEACHUM

Why, look ye, Mrs Di, you deal so hard with us that we can
afford to give the gentlemen who venture their lives for the
goods little or nothing.

MRS TRAPES

The hard times oblige me to go very near in my dealing. To be
sure, of late years I have been a great sufferer by the Parliament.   20
Three thousand pounds would hardly make me amends. The
Act for destroying the Mint was a severe cut upon our business.
Till then, if a customer stepped out of the way we knew where
to have her. No doubt you know Mrs Coaxer – there's a wench

12   *blacks* mourning clothes.
13   *mantoes* the manto(e), manteau or (most commonly) mantua was a woman's loose
        gown. Often of rich material, elaborately embroidered, and worn open at the front
        over a petticoat, it was fashionable for wear on all social occasions until the 1750s.
14   *chap* buyer, customer.
14–15   *very fond of mourning* because mourning clothes made them look respectable and
        were often made of expensive fabrics. In better-off families, widows were expected
        to wear mourning for two years or more. During the eighteenth century, public
        mourning for members of the royal family was seen as a sign of social status and
        increasingly observed by the middling as well as the upper classes. Many
        Londoners wore mourning after the death of George I in June 1727.
22   *Act . . . Mint* an Act of Parliament which came into force in 1723 to enforce the rule
        of law in the Mint, an area of Southwark notorious as a haven for criminals.

now (till today) with a good suit of clothes of mine upon her   25
back, and I could never set eyes upon her for three months
together. Since the Act too against imprisonment for small
sums, my loss there too hath been very considerable, and it must
be so, when a lady can borrow a handsome petticoat, or a clean
gown, and I not have the least hank upon her! And, o' my   30
conscience, nowadays most ladies take a delight in cheating,
when they can do it with safety.

PEACHUM

Madam, you had a handsome gold watch of us t'other day for
seven guineas. Considering we must have our profit, to a
gentleman upon the road a gold watch will be scarce worth the   35
taking.

MRS TRAPES

Consider, Mr Peachum, that watch was remarkable, and not of
very safe sale. If you have any black velvet scarfs, they are a
handsome winter wear, and take with most gentlemen who deal
with my customers. 'Tis I that put the ladies upon a good foot.   40
'Tis not youth or beauty that fixes their price. The gentlemen
always pay according to their dress, from half a crown to two
guineas; and yet those hussies make nothing of bilking of me.
Then too, allowing for accidents – I have eleven fine customers
now down under the surgeon's hands – what with fees and other   45
expenses, there are great goings-out and no comings-in, and not
a farthing to pay for at least a month's clothing. We run great
risks, great risks indeed.

PEACHUM

As I remember, you said something just now of Mrs Coaxer.

MRS TRAPES

Yes, sir. To be sure, I stripped her of a suit of my own clothes   50
about two hours ago, and have left her as she should be, in her
shift, with a lover of hers at my house. She called him upstairs as

---

27–8 *Act . . . sums* an Act of Parliament which came into force in 1726, preventing
       imprisonment for debts of less than £10 in a superior or £40 in an inferior court.
       Before the Act, Mrs. Trapes would have been able to have customers who owed her
       comparatively small amounts of money imprisoned for debt.
30 *hank* hold.
37 *remarkable* unusual, noticeable.
43 *bilking* cheating.
45 *down . . . hands* because they are suffering from venereal disease. Compare note to
       I.ii.24–5.

he was going to Marybone in a hackney coach. And I hope, for
her own sake and mine, she will persuade the Captain to redeem
her, for the Captain is very generous to the ladies.   55

LOCKIT

What Captain?

MRS TRAPES

He thought I did not know him – an intimate acquaintance of
yours, Mr Peachum – only Captain Macheath, as fine as a lord.

PEACHUM

Tomorrow, dear Mrs Di, you shall set your own price upon any
of the goods you like. We have at least half a dozen velvet scarfs,   60
and all at your service. Will you give me leave to make you a
present of the suit of nightclothes for your own wearing? But
are you sure it is Captain Macheath?

MRS TRAPES

Though he thinks I have forgotten him, nobody knows him
better. I have taken a great deal of the Captain's money in my   65
time at second hand, for he always loved to have his ladies well
dressed.

PEACHUM

Mr Lockit and I have a little business with the Captain – you
understand me – and we will satisfy you for Mrs Coaxer's debt.

LOCKIT

Depend upon it; we will deal like men of honour.   70

MRS TRAPES

I don't enquire after your affairs, so whatever happens, I wash
my hands on't. It hath always been my maxim that one friend
should assist another. But if you please, I'll take one of the scarfs
home with me. 'Tis always good to have something in hand.

[*Exeunt*]

---

53   *hackney coach* a hired carriage.
62   *nightclothes* informal evening wear.

[ACT III,] SCENE vii

[Scene,] Newgate

[Enter] LUCY

LUCY

Jealousy, rage, love, and fear are at once tearing me to pieces.
How I am weather-beaten and shattered with distresses!

Air 47   One Evening having Lost my Way   [Anon]

LUCY

I'm like a skiff on the ocean tossed,
    Now high, now low, with each billow borne,
With her rudder broke, and her anchor lost,   5
    Deserted and all forlorn.
While thus I lie rolling and tossing all night,
That Polly lies sporting on seas of delight!
        Revenge, revenge, revenge,
    Shall appease my restless sprite.   10

1 *Jealousy . . . pieces* This begins the parody of Italian opera's heightened language
   and sentiment which runs through the next three scenes.
2 *Air 47 One . . . Way* The title is the first line of a ballad entitled 'The Happy Clown'.
   In the third edition of *The Dancing Master* (1718), 2. 347, it is printed as 'Wallpoole;
   or the happy clown'. The tune was used by Pepusch in his overture, and there may
   have been deliberate allusion to Walpole in the selection.

LUCY

I have the ratsbane ready. I run no risk; for I can lay her death
upon the gin, and so many die of that naturally that I shall never
be called in question. But say I were to be hanged – I never could
be hanged for anything that would give me greater comfort than
the poisoning that slut.   15

Enter FILCH

FILCH

Madam, here's Miss Polly come to wait upon you.

LUCY

Show her in.   [*Exit* FILCH]

[ACT III,] SCENE viii

LUCY [*remains; to her enter*] POLLY

LUCY

Dear madam, your servant. I hope you will pardon my passion
when I was so happy to see you last. I was so over-run with the
spleen that I was perfectly out of myself. And really when one
hath the spleen, everything is to be excused by a friend.

Air 48   Now Roger, I'll Tell Thee, Because Thou'rt my Son   [Anon]

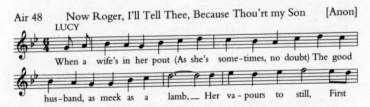

When a wife's in her pout (As she's some-times, no doubt) The good
hus-band, as meek as a lamb,— Her va-pours to still, First

11   *I . . . ready* Cups of poisoned cordial appear in a number of Handel's operas.
Ratsbane is rat poison.

11–12   *lay . . . naturally* Gin was readily and cheaply available and became the drink of the
poor, but it was often of very poor quality, even poisonous, so that deaths in gin
shops were not uncommon.

1   *passion* angry outburst.

2–3   *the spleen* The spleen was thought to be the seat of various moods and nervous
disorders and was the subject of several treatises, both learned and popular, in the
1720s. Suffering from 'the spleen' became a fashionable condition, particularly for
women, and was associated with refined feeling and sometimes intelligence.

4   *Air 48 Now . . . Son* No contemporary source for the tune or the words has been
located. The melody to the words 'Her vapours to' is, as in Barlow, taken from O1,
O2, since it fits the bass of Q1 better than the notes printed there.

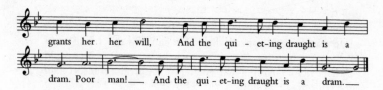

grants her her will, And the qui - et-ing draught is a
dram. Poor man!___ And the qui - et-ing draught is a dram.___

LUCY

When a wife's in her pout   5
(As she's sometimes, no doubt)
   The good husband, as meek as a lamb,
     Her vapours to still,
     First grants her her will,
   And the quieting draught is a dram.   10
Poor man! And the quieting draught is a dram.

LUCY

I wish all our quarrels might have so comfortable a recon-
ciliation.

POLLY

I have no excuse for my own behaviour, madam, but my
misfortunes – and really, madam, I suffer too upon your   15
account.

LUCY

But, Miss Polly, in the way of friendship, will you give me leave
to propose a glass of cordial to you?

POLLY

Strong waters are apt to give me the headache. I hope, madam,
you will excuse me.   20

LUCY

Not the greatest lady in the land could have better in her closet
for her own private drinking. You seem mighty low in spirits,
my dear.

POLLY

I am sorry, madam, my health will not allow me to accept of
your offer. I should not have left you in the rude manner I did   25
when we met last, madam, had not my papa hauled me away so
unexpectedly. I was indeed somewhat provoked, and perhaps

   5   *pout* sulky mood.
   8   *vapours* depression, ill humour.
  10   *a dram* a measure of spirits.
  21   *closet* private room.

might use some expressions that were disrespectful. But really, madam, the Captain treated me with so much contempt and cruelty that I deserved your pity rather than your resentment.   30

LUCY

But since his escape, no doubt all matters are made up again. Ah Polly, Polly! 'Tis I am the unhappy wife; and he loves you as if you were only his mistress.

POLLY

Sure, madam, you cannot think me so happy as to be the object of your jealousy. A man is always afraid of a woman who loves   35 him too well, so that I must expect to be neglected and avoided.

LUCY

Then our cases, my dear Polly, are exactly alike. Both of us indeed have been too fond.

Air 49   Oh Bessy Bell   [Anon]

POLLY

A curse attends that woman's love
    Who always would be pleasing.   40

LUCY

The pertness of the billing dove,
    Like tickling, is but teasing.

POLLY

What then in love can woman do?

38   *Air 49 O . . . Bell* The first line of a ballad by Allan Ramsay issued in 1724 in which the speaker is unable to choose between two women, Bessy Bell and Mary Gray. The tune is considerably older.

41   *pertness* boldness.

LUCY

If we grow fond they shun us.

POLLY

And when we fly them, they pursue,   45

LUCY

But leave us when they've won us.

LUCY

Love is so very whimsical in both sexes that it is impossible to be lasting. But my heart is particular, and contradicts my own observation.

POLLY

But really, Mistress Lucy, by his last behaviour, I think I ought to   50
envy you. When I was forced from him, he did not show the least
tenderness. But perhaps, he hath a heart not capable of it.

Air 50   Would Fate to me Belinda Give   [John Wilford]

POLLY
A-mong the men, co-quets we find, Who court by
turns all wo-man-kind; And we grant all their
hearts de-sired, When they are flat-tered, when they are
flat-tered, when they are flat-tered and ad-mired.

POLLY

Among the men, coquets we find,
Who court by turns all womankind;
And we grant all their hearts desired,   55
When they are flattered and admired.

POLLY

The coquets of both sexes are self-lovers, and that is a love no
other whatever can dispossess. I fear, my dear Lucy, our husband
is one of those.

48   *particular* attached just to one person.
52   *Air 50 Would ... Give* The first line on a song sheet of c. 1705 where the words are attri-
      buted to Mrs Mary Child. It is a song of simple adoration. The tune is by John Wilford.
53   *coquets* flirts.

LUCY

Away with these melancholy reflections! Indeed, my dear Polly, 60
we are both of us a cup too low – let me prevail upon you to
accept of my offer.

Air 51   Come, Sweet Lass   [Anon]

LUCY
Come, sweet lass, Let's ban-ish so-row Till to-mor-row;
Come, sweet lass, Let's take a chirp-ing glass.
Wine can clear The va-pours of des-pair And
make us light as air; Then drink, and ban—ish— care.

LUCY

Come, sweet lass,
Let's banish sorrow
Till tomorrow;   65
Come, sweet lass,
Let's take a chirping glass.
Wine can clear
The vapours of despair
And make us light as air;   70
Then drink, and banish care.

LUCY

I can't bear, child, to see you in such low spirits, and I must
persuade you to what I know will do you good. (*Aside*) I shall
now soon be even with the hypocritical strumpet.   [*Exit*]

---

61   *a cup too low* in need of a drink.
62   *Air 51 Come, Sweet Lass* The first line of a broadside entitled 'An Excellent New
     Scotch Song . . . Lately Sung in a New Play at the Royal Theatre'.
67   *chirping* cheering.

[ACT III,] SCENE ix

POLLY [*remains, alone*]

POLLY

All this wheedling of Lucy cannot be for nothing – at this time too, when I know she hates me! – The dissembling of a woman is always the forerunner of mischief. – By pouring strong waters down my throat, she thinks to pump some secrets out of me. I'll be upon my guard, and won't taste a drop of her liquor, I'm resolved.   5

[ACT III,] SCENE x

POLLY [*remains; to her enter*] LUCY, *with strong waters*

LUCY

Come, Miss Polly.

POLLY

Indeed, child, you have given yourself trouble to no purpose. – You must, my dear, excuse me.

LUCY

Really, Miss Polly, you are so squeamishly affected about taking a cup of strong waters as a lady before company. I vow, Polly, I   5
shall take it monstrously ill if you refuse me. Brandy and men (though women love them never so well) are always taken by us with some reluctance – unless 'tis in private.

POLLY

[*Taking a glass*] I protest, madam, it goes against me. – What do I see? Macheath again in custody! – Now every glimmering of   10
happiness is lost.

Drops the glass of liquor on the ground

LUCY

(*Aside*) Since things are thus, I'm glad the wench hath escaped; for by this event, 'tis plain, she was not happy enough to deserve to be poisoned.

11 s.d. *Drops . . . ground* A further parody of Italian opera in which the poison is often spilled before it can be drunk.
12 s.d. *Aside* O1; omitted O2, Q1.

[ACT III,] SCENE xi

LUCY [*and*] POLLY [*remain; to them enter*] LOCKIT,
[*and*] PEACHUM [*with*] MACHEATH [*in chains*]

LOCKIT

Set your heart to rest, Captain; you have neither the chance of
love or money for another escape, for you are ordered to be
called down upon your trial immediately.

PEACHUM

Away, hussies! This is not a time for a man to be hampered with
his wives. You see, the gentleman is in chains already.   5

LUCY

Oh husband, husband, my heart longed to see thee; but to see
thee thus distracts me.

POLLY

Will not my dear husband look upon his Polly? Why hadst thou
not flown to me for protection? With me thou hadst been safe.

Air 52   The Last Time I Went o'er the Moor   [Anon]

Hith-er, dear hus-band, turn your eyes. Be-stow one glance to cheer me.
Think with that look, thy Pol-ly dies. O shun me not, but hear me.
'Tis Pol-ly sues. 'Tis Lu-cy speaks. Is thus true love re-quit-ed?
My heart is burst-ing. Mine too breaks. Must I, Must I be slight-ed?

0   This is the scene which Hogarth depicted in a painting of which five versions
survive.

9   *Air 52 The . . . Moor* The first line of a poem by Allan Ramsay, entitled 'The Happy
Lover's Reflections' first published in 1724 in *Tea Table Miscellany*, p. 74. The tune
appeared in *Orpheus Caledonius*, 1725. It is not there a duet but a straightforward
assertion of a man's loyalty to his sweetheart.

POLLY   Hither, dear husband, turn your eyes.   10
LUCY   Bestow one glance to cheer me.
POLLY   Think with that look, thy Polly dies.
LUCY   O shun me not, but hear me.
POLLY   'Tis Polly sues.
LUCY   'Tis Lucy speaks.
POLLY   Is thus true love requited?   15
LUCY   My heart is bursting.
POLLY   Mine too breaks.
LUCY   Must I,
POLLY   Must I be slighted?

MACHEATH

What would you have me say, ladies? You see, this affair will
soon be at an end, without my disobliging either of you.

PEACHUM

But the settling this point, Captain, might prevent a law suit   20
between your two widows.

Air 53   Tom Tinker's my True Love   [Anon]

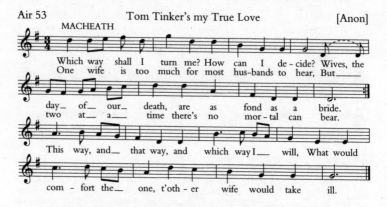

MACHEATH

Which way shall I turn me? How can I decide?
Wives, the day of our death, are as fond as a bride.

21   *Air 53 Tom . . . Sweetheart* Though a tune, 'Tom Tinker', dates back to the early 17th
century, the version of the tune in the opera comes from *Pills*, 6, p. 265, set to a
ballad whose obscene rhymes are indicated by a dash. It would have been strongly
recalled by the fact that Gay's fifth line is an exact quotation from the original,
where it refers to sexual intercourse.

One wife is too much for most husbands to hear,
But two at a time there's no mortal can bear.   25
This way, and that way, and which way I will,
What would comfort the one, t'other wife would take ill.

POLLY

But if his own misfortunes have made him insensible to mine, a
father sure will be more compassionate. Dear, dear sir, sink the
material evidence, and bring him off at his trial. [*Kneeling*] Polly   30
upon her knees begs it of you.

Air 54   I am a Poor Shepherd Undone   [Anon]

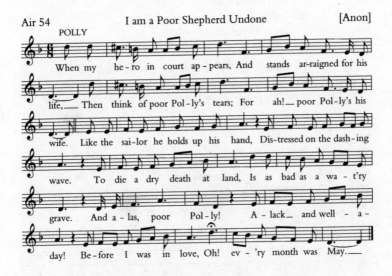

22   *Which way . . . me* Macheath's choice between Polly and Lucy burlesques that of
      various classical heroes. The Judgement of Hercules, a favourite subject of poets
      and painters, described Hercules's choice between pleasure and virtue, represented
      by two contrasting women. Marc Antony's choice between duty, to his wife
      Octavia, and desire, for Cleopatra, was familiar from both Shakespeare's *Antony
      and Cleopatra* and John Dryden's version, *All for Love* (1677). Macheath echoes
      Marc Antony's 'Oh . . . which way shall I turn' in Act III of Dryden's play. Hogarth's
      painting positions Macheath between the two women, emphasising his dilemma.
29   *sink* pass over in silence (*OED* 25b).
31   *Air 54 I . . . Undone* The seventeenth-century tune is known by several titles; it
      became associated with a popular song entitled 'The Distress'd Shepherd' of which
      this is the first line. The song is the lament of a rejected lover, and the last four lines
      of Polly's song are an almost exact quotation of the original.

POLLY

When my hero in court appears,
   And stands arraigned for his life,
Then think of poor Polly's tears;
   For ah! poor Polly's his wife.   35
Like the sailor he holds up his hand,
   Distressed on the dashing wave.
To die a dry death at land,
   Is as bad as a wat'ry grave.
And alas, poor Polly!   40
Alack, and well-a-day!
Before I was in love,
   Oh! ev'ry month was May.

LUCY

([*To* LOCKIT] *kneeling*) If Peachum's heart is hardened, sure
you, sir, will have more compassion on a daughter. I know the   45
evidence is in your power. How then can you be a tyrant to me?

Air 55   Ianthe the Lovely   [John Barrett]

When he holds up his hand arraigned for his life, O think of your daughter, and think I'm his wife! What are cannons, or bombs, or clashing of swords? For death is more certain by witnesses' words. Then nail up their lips; that dread thunder allay; And each month of my life, and each month of my life will hereafter be May.

LUCY

When he holds up his hand arraigned for his life,
O think of your daughter, and think I'm his wife!

44   s.d. *kneeling* This ed. Placed after Lucy's speech in original texts. Often directions
     are placed at the end of the speech to which they apply, and here Lucy might deliver
     her speech or her song, or both, on her knees, as Hogarth depicts her.
46   *Air 55 Ianthe the Lovely* The words of the original are by John Glanville (c. 1705),
     and the tune by John Barrett. It was first published c. 1706.

What are cannons, or bombs, or clashing of swords?
For death is more certain by witnesses' words.   50
Then nail up their lips; that dread thunder allay;
And each month of my life will hereafter be May.

LOCKIT

Macheath's time is come, Lucy. We know our own affairs,
therefore let us have no more whimpering or whining.

Air 56   A Cobbler There Was   [Anon]

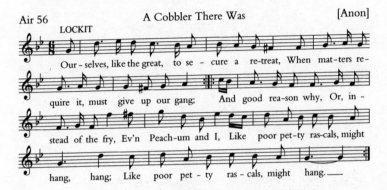

LOCKIT

Ourselves, like the great, to secure a retreat,   55
When matters require it, must give up our gang;
    And good reason why,
    Or, instead of the fry,
    Ev'n Peachum and I,
Like poor petty rascals, might hang, hang;   60
Like poor petty rascals, might hang.

PEACHUM

Set your heart at rest, Polly. Your husband is to die today.
Therefore if you are not already provided, 'tis high time to look
about for another. There's comfort for you, you slut.

LOCKIT

We are ready, sir, to conduct you to the Old Bailey.   65

---

54 *Air 56 A . . . Was* Though the tune, known by various names, was in circulation
    before 1700, the version used here, called 'The Cobler's End', was not printed until
    1729.
58 *fry* inferior beings (literally, young fish produced in large numbers).

Air 57   Bonny Dundee   [Anon]

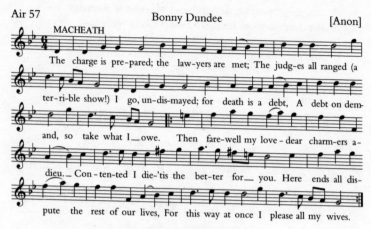

MACHEATH

The charge is prepared; the lawyers are met;
The judges all ranged (a terrible show!)
I go, undismayed; for death is a debt,
A debt on demand, so take what I owe.
Then farewell my love – dear charmers, adieu.   70
Contented I die – 'tis the better for you.
Here ends all dispute the rest of our lives,
For this way at once I please all my wives.

MACHEATH

Now, gentlemen, I am ready to attend you.

[*Exeunt* MACHEATH, LOCKIT, PEACHUM]

[ACT III,] SCENE xii

LUCY [*and*] POLLY [*remain; to them enter*] FILCH

POLLY

Follow them, Filch, to the court. And when the trial is over,

65   *Air 57 Bonny Dundee* A seventeenth-century tune to a ballad about a man's escape
from Dundee where he has got a minister's daughter pregnant – an appropriately
ironic commentary on Macheath's situation.

bring me a particular account of his behaviour, and of everything that happened – you'll find me here with Miss Lucy.

(*Exit* FILCH)

[*Music heard offstage*]

But why is all this music?

LUCY

The prisoners whose trials are put off till next session, are 5
diverting themselves.

POLLY

Sure there is nothing so charming as music; I'm fond of it to distraction! But, alas! Now, all mirth seems an insult upon my affliction. Let us retire, my dear Lucy, and indulge our sorrows. The noisy crew, you see, are coming upon us. 10

Exeunt

A dance of prisoners in chains, etc

[ACT III,] SCENE xiii

[*Scene,*] *the condemned hold*

MACHEATH, *in a melancholy posture*

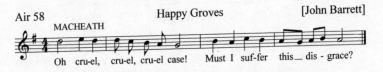

Air 58   Happy Groves   [John Barrett]

MACHEATH

Oh cru-el, cru-el, cru-el case! Must I suf-fer this— dis-grace?

III.xii   This narratively extraneous scene may be included in part to signal the passing of the time of Macheath's court appearance; more practically, it gives time for Macheath to leave the stage and make his way to the scene of the condemned hold.

2   *particular* precise, detailed.

3   s.d. *Music . . . offstage* ed. No music is given in the original editions.

10   s.d. *A dance . . . chains* burlesquing the more elegant ballets and other dances included in performances of Italian opera. It is often omitted in modern productions. *etc.* This presumably implies that the prisoners are fettered in various ways, with handcuffs, leg-irons and the rest.

1–29   This sequence of songs poses a number of questions about the manner of its performance, since the music does not link together straightforwardly. Many later

O cruel, cruel, cruel case!
Must I suffer this disgrace?

Air 59   Of All the Girls that are so Smart   [Henry Carey]

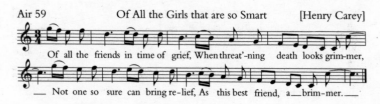

Of all the friends in time of grief, When threat'-ning death looks grim-mer,
— Not one so sure can bring re-lief, As this best friend, a—brim-mer.—

Of all the friends in time of grief,
When threat'ning death looks grimmer,
Not one so sure can bring relief,   5
As this best friend, a brimmer.   (*Drinks*)

Air 60   Britons Strike Home   [Henry Purcell]

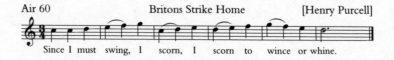

Since I must swing, I scorn, I scorn to wince or whine.

Since I must swing, I scorn, I scorn to wince or whine.   (*Rises*)

Air 61   Chevy Chase   [Anon]

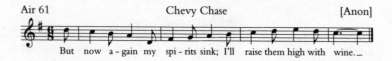

But now a-gain my spi-rits sink; I'll raise them high with wine.—

arrangers have attempted to stitch the fragments musically together, but Barlow, ed., p. xi, concludes that they 'were . . . sung just as they stand . . . the abruptness of the changes is intended to underline Macheath's rapid swings of mood'.

0   *Air 58 Happy Groves* The title of a song in Vanbrugh's comedy, *The Pilgrim* (1700), to music by John Barrett. It celebrates a lover's joy, making a straightforward ironic contrast with Macheath's situation.

3   *Air 59 Of All . . . Smart* The first line of the song entitled 'Salley in our Alley', one of the most popular of Henry Carey's airs, first issued c. 1715. Macheath's lyric saluting drink imitates the structure of the original's praise of 'Salley'.

6   *brimmer* a full glass.
     Air 60 Britons . . . Home The first line of a warlike song in the tragedy *Bonduca* (1695), to a Purcell tune.

7   *Air 61 Chevy Chase* One of the most often mentioned of ballad tunes. It is prescribed for such a wide variety of lyrics that there is unlikely to be any specific recall here. The version of the tune in O1, O2 has an effective dotted crotchet rest after 'sink'.

But now again my spirits sink;
I'll raise them high with wine. (*Drinks a glass of wine*)

Air 62   To Old Simon the King   [Anon]

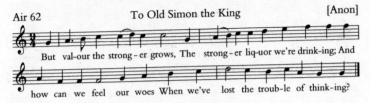

But valour the stronger grows, The stronger liquor we're drinking; And
how can we feel our woes When we've lost the trouble of thinking?

But valour the stronger grows,   10
The stronger liquor we're drinking;
And how can we feel our woes
When we've lost the trouble of thinking?   (*Drinks*)

Air 63   Joy to Great Caesar   [Michael Farinelli]

If thus— a man can die Much bold-er with bran-dy.

If thus – A man can die
Much bolder with brandy.   15
    (*Pours out a bumper of brandy*)

Air 64   There was an Old Woman   [Anon]

So I drink off this bumper.— And now I can stand the test.— And my
com-rades shall see that I die as brave as the best.—

So I drink off this bumper. – And now I can stand the test.
And my comrades shall see that I die as brave as the best.
                                Drinks

9   *Air 62 To Old . . . King* Another very widely used tune, dating back at least to the
early seventeenth century. Though political ballads were set to it, these do not seem
to be recalled in any specific way here.

13   *Air 63 Joy . . . Caesar* The first line of a poem by D'Urfey of which the first stanza
is a toast to Charles II, set to a version of an old tune, 'La Folia'. The dashes in this
and the subsequent airs may suggest a pause or hold as Macheath drinks.

15   *Air 64 There . . . Woman* Many ballad lyrics begin with this phrase; the tune is
known as 'Puddings and Pies'.

Air 65   Did you Ever Hear of a Gallant Sailor   [Anon]

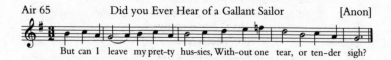

But can I leave my pret-ty hus-sies, With-out one tear, or ten-der sigh?

> But can I leave my pretty hussies,
> Without one tear, or tender sigh?

Air 66   Why are mine Eyes Still Flowing   [Anon]

Their eyes, their   lips,   their   bus – – – – – ses

Re - call   my   love.—   Ah,   must   I___   die?

> Their eyes, their lips, their busses   20
> Recall my love. – Ah, must I die?

Air 67   Greensleeves   [Anon]

Since   laws were made for ev-'ry de-gree,   To   curb vice in oth-ers, as

well   as me,   I   won-der we han't bet-ter   com - pa-ny Up-on

Ty -   burn tree!___   But_   gold   from law_   can

take out the sting; And   if   rich men, like   us, were to swing, 'Twould

thin   the land, such num-bers to string Up-on   Ty - burn tree!__

17   *Air 65 Did . . . Sailor* The first line of a ballad lamenting the inconstancy of a sailor's beloved, to a tune called 'The unconstant woman', published 1707, though words and tune may be older.

19   *Air 66 Why . . . Flowing* The first line of a lyric by D'Urfey in praise of his beloved, first issued in 1687.

20   *busses* kisses.

21   *Air 67 Greensleeves* One of the best known of all ballad tunes, dating back at least to the sixteenth century, and surviving in different forms, with different names, and associated with ballads of many kinds, including political satire.

Since laws were made for ev'ry degree,
To curb vice in others, as well as me,
I wonder we han't better company
        Upon Tyburn tree!   25
But gold from law can take out the sting;
And if rich men, like us, were to swing,
'Twould thin the land, such numbers to string
        Upon Tyburn tree!

[*Enter* JAILER]

JAILER

Some friends of yours, Captain, desire to be admitted. I leave   30
you together.   [*Exit*]

[ACT III,] SCENE xiv

MACHEATH [*remains; to him enter*] BEN BUDGE,
        MATT OF THE MINT

MACHEATH

For my having broke prison, you see, gentlemen, I am ordered
immediate execution. The sheriff's officers, I believe, are now at
the door. That Jemmy Twitcher should peach me, I own
surprised me! 'Tis a plain proof that the world is all alike, and
that even our gang can no more trust one another than other   5
people. Therefore, I beg you, gentlemen, look well to yourselves,
for in all probability you may live some months longer.

MATT OF THE MINT

We are heartily sorry, Captain, for your misfortune – but 'tis
what we must all come to.

MACHEATH

Peachum and Lockit, you know, are infamous scoundrels. Their   10
lives are as much in your power as yours are in theirs. Remember
your dying friend! 'Tis my last request: bring those villains to the
gallows before you, and I am satisfied.

---

3   *peach* betray.

MATT OF THE MINT
We'll do it.

[*Enter* JAILER]

JAILER
Miss Polly and Miss Lucy entreat a word with you.   15
MACHEATH
Gentlemen, adieu.

[*Exeunt* BEN BUDGE, MATT OF THE MINT]

[ACT III,] SCENE xv

MACHEATH [*remains; to him enter*] LUCY, POLLY

MACHEATH
My dear Lucy – my dear Polly. Whatsoever hath passed between
us is now at an end. If you are fond of marrying again, the best
advice I can give you is to ship yourselves off for the West Indies,
where you'll have a fair chance of getting a husband apiece, or,
by good luck, two or three, as you like best.   5
POLLY
How can I support this sight!
LUCY
There is nothing moves one so much as a great man in distress.

Air 68   All You that Must Take a Leap   [Lewis Ramondon]

Would I might be hanged! And I would so too! To be
hanged with you. My dear, with you. Oh leave me to thought! I

2   *fond of* eager to.
3   *ship . . . West Indies* Women were under-represented in the colonies. *Polly* (1730),
     Gay's sequel to *The Beggar's Opera*, is set in the West Indies.
7   *Air 67 All . . . Leap* The first line of a lyric entitled 'A hymn upon the execution of
     two criminals' published, with a tune by Lewis Ramondon, c. 1710. It resonates
     with Gay's lyric, but he allocates the tune to the three principals, with their very
     different perspectives, imitating the frequent use of ensemble numbers at dramatic
     climaxes in Italian opera. The chorus to the words 'tol de rol' mentioned in the text

fear!— I doubt! I trem-ble! I droop! See, my cou-rage is out! No

MACHEATH   LUCY   POLLY

to-ken of love? See, my cou-rage is out. No to-ken of love?— A-

LUCY   POLLY   LUCY   POLLY

dieu.— Fare - well. No to - ken of_ love? A - dieu.— Fare -

MACHEATH

well. But hark!— I hear_ the_ toll of the bell.

LUCY	Would I might be hanged!
POLLY	And I would so too!
LUCY	To be hanged with you.
POLLY	My dear, with you.
MACHEATH	Oh leave me to thought! I fear! I doubt!

10

I tremble! I droop! See, my courage is out!

Turns up the empty bottle

POLLY	No token of love?
MACHEATH	See, my courage is out.

Turns up the empty pot

LUCY	No token of love?
POLLY	Adieu.
LUCY	Farewell.
MACHEATH	But hark! I hear the toll of the bell.
CHORUS	Tol de rol lol, etc.

15

[*Enter* JAILER]

JAILER

Four women more, Captain, with a child apiece! See, here they come.

is not indicated in the musical score, and is it not clear who sings it – the three characters on stage, or an off-stage group imitating the tolling of the bell. It is also not obvious how much of the music is repeated to this chorus. Barlow, ed., suggests that it might repeat the last eight bars and a beat, and repeat also the words of the last line.

19   *toll . . . bell* The bell of St Sepulchre's church near Newgate began to toll five minutes before a condemned criminal emerged for the final journey to execution at Tyburn. Lewis, ed., suggests that Gay recalls and parodies the end of Otway's tragedy, *Venice Preserved*, where a tolling bell heralds Pierre's execution.

113

Enter women and children

MACHEATH

What – four wives more! This is too much. Here – tell the sheriff's officers I am ready.

Exit MACHEATH *guarded*

[ACT III,] SCENE xvi

To them, enter PLAYER *and* BEGGAR

PLAYER

But, honest friend, I hope you don't intend that Macheath shall be really executed.

BEGGAR

Most certainly, sir. To make the piece perfect, I was for doing strict poetical justice. Macheath is to be hanged; and for the other personages of the drama, the audience must have supposed they were all hanged or transported.

PLAYER

Why then, friend, this is a downright deep tragedy. The catastrophe is manifestly wrong, for an opera must end happily.

BEGGAR

Your objection, sir, is very just, and is easily removed. For you must allow that in this kind of drama 'tis no matter how absurdly things are brought about. – So, you rabble there, run and cry a reprieve. Let the prisoner be brought back to his wives in triumph.

PLAYER

All this we must do to comply with the taste of the town.

BEGGAR

Through the whole piece you may observe such a similitude of manners in high and low life, that it is difficult to determine whether, in the fashionable vices, the fine gentlemen imitate the gentlemen of the road, or the gentlemen of the road, the fine gentlemen. Had the play remained as I at first intended, it would

---

4   *strict poetical justice* according to which, virtue is rewarded and vice punished.
10-11   *this kind . . . brought about* Referring either to *The Beggar's Opera* itself, which is very difficult to categorise generically (see Introduction, p. viii-xiv), or to Italian opera, notorious for its contrived happy endings.

have carried a most excellent moral. 'Twould have shown that   20
the lower sort of people have their vices in a degree as well as the
rich, and that they are punished for them.

[ACT III,] SCENE xvii

To them, MACHEATH *with rabble, etc*

MACHEATH

So, it seems, I am not left to my choice, but must have a wife at
last. Look ye, my dears, we will have no controversy now. Let us
give this day to mirth, and I am sure she who thinks herself my
wife will testify her joy by a dance.

ALL

Come, a dance, a dance!   5

MACHEATH

Ladies, I hope you will give me leave to present a partner to each
of you. And (if I may without offence) for this time, I take Polly
for mine. [*To* POLLY] And for life, you slut – for we were really
married. As for the rest – but at present keep your own secret.

A Dance

Air 69   Lumps of Pudding   [Anon]

MACHEATH

Thus I stand like the Turk, with his dox-ies a-round; From
all sides their glan-ces his pas-sion con-found; For black, brown, and
fair, his in-con-stan-cy burns, And the dif-fer-ent beau-ties sub –

0 s.d. *etc.* This presumably indicates that all the cast participate in the final dance.
1 *not left ... choice* which, he claims, would be to hang rather than be married.
9 s.d. *A Dance* There are many possibilities in performance for incorporating the
   dance and song. The performers might initially dance to the passages marked for
   the violin, but it would be easy to repeat the tune many times over.
   Air 69 Lumps of Pudding The title of a tune to a comic bawdy lyric beginning 'When I
   was in the low country'. It is found in a variant form in *The Dancing Master* (1701 ed.).

115

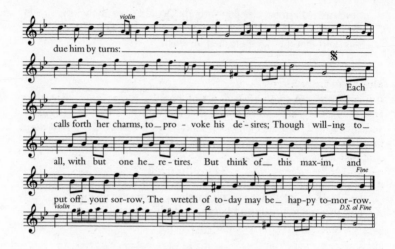

MACHEATH

Thus I stand like the Turk, with his doxies around;   10
From all sides their glances his passion confound;
For black, brown, and fair, his inconstancy burns,
And the different beauties subdue him by turns:
Each calls forth her charms, to provoke his desires;
Though willing to all, with but one he retires.   15
But think of this maxim, and put off your sorrow,
The wretch of today may be happy tomorrow.

CHORUS

But think of this maxim, and put off your sorrow,
The wretch of today may be happy tomorrow.

FINIS

10   *like the Turk . . . doxies* referring either to Turkish men in general, whose tradition of polygamy was commonly invoked at this period in order to assert the superiority of Christian cultures; or, more particularly, to the Turkish Sultan and his harem of slave women. Doxies are mistresses of criminals, hence prostitutes (see commentary on Dramatis Personae).

APPENDIX

Music and Composers

It is convenient to speak of Gay's use of 'popular' music in *The Beggar's Opera*, and to do so is to recognise that most, if not all, of the original audience would have been relatively familiar with most, if not all, of the tunes they heard. But it is important not to let the label 'popular' become confused with what we now denote by the term. Though many of the melodies Gay adopted had a long history, some going back to the sixteenth century or even before, and so might be seen as genuinely 'popular', others came from relatively recent theatrical performances or published song sheets, and yet others were taken from the works of eminent 'serious' composers. The boundaries between 'high' and 'popular' music were constituted very differently in the eighteenth century.

Exactly how Gay came to know and to select the tunes for which his lyrics were composed cannot be determined for certain. Some must simply have been 'in the air', circulating in various forms and attached to a variety of ballad texts. Gay might have found the tunes for many of his songs written down in a number of places, including the massive collection of lyrics and tunes made by Thomas D'Urfey (see below), but he could equally well have drawn them from single-sheet publications, or from sources such as Playford's *The Dancing Master*, which went through many editions from the 1650s to 1728, or, if he was indeed a flautist or recorder player, from other instrumental sources including *The Bird Fancyer's Delight* (1717).

The most exhaustive general survey of ballads and their music is that by Claude M. Simpson in *The British Broadside Ballad and its Music*, 1966, where much more detailed information than can possibly be included in the notes to this edition may be found. Jeremy Barlow's edition of the music summarises what is known of the specific sources for Gay's tunes. The biographies of those musicians known to have composed the originals of individual airs are given below.

John Barrett (c. 1676–1719). Organist, and music master at Christ's Hospital. Most of his composition was for the theatre.

Giovanni Buononcini (also spelt Bononcini) (1670–1747). Italian opera composer. His opera, *Camilla*, in an English translation, had been an early eighteenth-century 'hit' at the same theatre as Gay's work. Best known today as Handel's operatic rival.

Henry Carey (1687–1743). Poet and composer, particularly significant in his attempts, with others, to establish English opera, and for his satires of Italian operatic forms. He published at least 250 songs during the period 1710–40.

Jeremiah Clarke (c. 1674–1707). Chorister, organist, and composer of music both for the church and for the theatre. Best known today for the so-called 'Trumpet Voluntary' or 'Prince of Denmark's March'.

Thomas D'Urfey (?1653–1723). Writer, playwright and singer. During his latter years he collected his own lyrics, and those of others in *Wit and Mirth: or Pills to Purge Melancholy*, published by Playford in steadily expanding editions between 1698 and 1720. Many of the tunes used by Gay are to be found in this collection, which, like the *Opera*, mixes street ballad with more sophisticated poetry, and tunes dating back centuries with the latest songs from the theatre.

John Eccles (?1668–1735) A significant composer, both for the theatre (he was for a time musical director at the Theatre Royal, Lincoln's Inn Fields), and for the court, notable especially for the quality of his songs.

John Freeman (1666–1736). Primarily a singer, known to have performed in a number of Purcell's works. He composed several songs published during the 1690s, of which 'Pretty Parrot' is the only one to have achieved longevity through its adoption by Gay.

George Frideric Handel (1685–1759). Born in Germany, Handel arrived in England in 1710, and was later naturalised. He was the major figure in the musical life of the country, initially as an opera composer, but also as provider of music for the court and for the church. His oratorios became a staple of English choral music. Gay wrote the libretto for his secular cantata, *Acis and Galatea* (1717), and relations between the two men seem to have been cordial.

Richard Leveridge (1670–1758). A singer and theatrical performer who had a long and varied career. He sang, for example, in a number of Purcell compositions, and in the first performance of Handel's *Acis and Galatea*. He composed music for Shakespeare's *Macbeth* which remained in use until well into the nineteenth century.

Johann Christian Pepusch (1667–1752). Composer, theorist, violinist and theatrical musical director. Born in Germany, but settled in England, he was a considerable musical presence, composing both sacred and secular music, and, like many musicians, earning a living for much of his career as musical director in various theatres. He is sometimes credited with choosing the music for *The Beggar's Opera*, but this is very unlikely. He did, however, certainly compose the overture and arranged the tunes for the first performance, and for publication in Q1.

Henry Purcell (1659–95). The most distinguished composer of his time, and one of the greatest in the whole history of English music. He was an organist, a court composer, and worked, especially in the last years of his life, in the theatre. His output covers solo songs, instrumental works, anthems and large-scale choral compositions as well as theatrical works which contributed to the establishment of opera in England.

Lewis [Littleton] Ramondon (1684– c. 1715). A theatrical performer, singer and composer whose songs, mostly written for the theatre, appeared in various forms.

Pietro Sandoni Little is known of him except that he was married to the opera singer Francesca Cuzzoni.

George Vanbrugh A bass singer and composer who published three volumes of songs, and a little instrumental music. He may have been related to the architect sir John Vanbrugh.

John Wilford A composer of whom virtually nothing is known. Barlow in his edition states that 'he had several songs published on single-sheets in the first twenty years of the 18th century' (p. 114).